Sourdough Discard Recipes Cookbook

Effortless, Zero-Waste Recipes for Busy Families. Transform Sourdough Discard into Wholesome, Time-Saving Meals Everyone Will Love!

Sara Dougherty

Table of Content:

Meet the Author

Hi there! I'm **Sara Dougherty**, a passionate home baker and advocate for sustainable, zero-waste cooking. For years, I've been experimenting in the kitchen, learning how to turn every bit of sourdough discard into something truly wonderful. My journey with sourdough began as a simple hobby, but it quickly grew into a passion as I realized just how much we can do with the ingredients we already have—without wasting a single crumb.

As a busy mom, I know firsthand how challenging it can be to prepare healthy, home-cooked meals for the family while juggling the demands of everyday life. That's why I've made it my mission to create recipes that are not only nutritious but also time-saving and practical for busy households like mine.

My approach to cooking is simple: food should be delicious, wholesome, and sustainable. I love the idea of turning what might be considered "scraps" into dishes that can nourish both body and soul. My hope is that this cookbook will inspire you to get creative in your kitchen, reduce waste, and make the most of your sourdough discard.

When I'm not baking, I enjoy spending time with my family, trying out new recipes, and sharing my experiences with the vibrant community of home bakers that has grown around me. I truly believe that with the right mindset and a little bit of creativity, anyone can transform their kitchen into a place of sustainability, joy, and delicious meals.

Thank you for joining me on this journey, and I can't wait to see how you bring these recipes to life in your own home!

Sara Dougherty

Chapter 1: Introduction – Welcome to Zero-Waste Cooking

Welcome to your sourdough adventure! Whether you're new to the world of sourdough baking or you're a seasoned pro looking to make the most of every scrap, this cookbook is your ultimate guide. We're going to take what many people might see as "waste" and turn it into something magical—meals that are both delicious and resourceful.

Cooking with sourdough discard isn't just about saving money or reducing waste (although those are fantastic perks!). It's about creating something meaningful in your kitchen. Each recipe in this book has been crafted with care to help you use up that sourdough discard in creative, unexpected ways. You'll transform a simple byproduct into pancakes, muffins, pizza crusts, and even desserts that your family will love. And the best part? No one will even guess they're eating "leftovers" from your starter!

The Journey from "Waste" to Wonder

Let's start with a quick truth: Sourdough baking can feel intimidating at first. You might think it requires too much time or effort. But here's a little secret: it's worth it. When you bake with sourdough, you're participating in a centuries-old tradition that celebrates patience, care, and sustainability.

But what about the discard? That pesky portion of your sourdough starter that you remove each time you feed it can feel like waste. You might wonder why you have to throw away part of something you've spent time cultivating. Well, the good news is that you don't have to waste a thing! This cookbook will show you how to use every bit of that discard to create meals that not only reduce waste but also bring exciting new flavors to your table.

Each time you pull a pancake off the griddle, take a bite of a warm muffin, or slice into a crispy pizza crust made with sourdough discard, you'll realize how satisfying it is to cook with intention and purpose. There's something deeply rewarding about knowing you're turning potential waste into something truly delightful.

What to Expect from This Cookbook

This isn't just another cookbook. It's a toolkit for anyone who wants to make the most out of their kitchen, while feeding their family in the healthiest, most sustainable way possible. Here's what you can look forward to:

- **190 Recipes to Inspire You:** Whether you're cooking breakfast, lunch, dinner, or dessert, there's a recipe in here that will use up your sourdough discard in the tastiest way.

- **Recipes for Every Occasion**: From quick, throw-together meals on busy weeknights to slow weekend brunches, you'll find dishes that fit every part of your schedule.

- **Zero-Waste Philosophy**: Each recipe in this book is designed to reduce waste and use every part of your sourdough starter. Even better, we'll include tips on how to apply this zero-waste mindset to other areas of your kitchen.

You'll also notice that the recipes are easy to follow. I've written them with busy lives in mind—because, let's be honest, not all of us have hours to spend in the kitchen. But that doesn't mean we can't make food that's worth savoring.

The Power of Sourdough Discard

Before we dive into the recipes, let's take a moment to understand why sourdough discard is so special. Discard is essentially part of the sourdough starter that you remove during feeding to keep the yeast culture healthy and manageable. While it might seem like a "leftover," it still contains all the incredible qualities that make sourdough unique: the natural fermentation, the depth of flavor, and the live, active cultures.

The real beauty of sourdough discard is that it doesn't need to go through a long fermentation process to be useful in recipes. It can add a subtle tang, richness, and complexity to everyday dishes—transforming them from ordinary to extraordinary with just one ingredient.

So, instead of seeing discard as a burden, think of it as an opportunity. An opportunity to be creative, resourceful, and a little adventurous in your cooking. In this book, you'll learn how to incorporate it into almost anything—from breakfast staples like pancakes and muffins to savory snacks, main courses, and even desserts.

How to Use This Cookbook

This book is organized to make your life easier. We'll start with the essentials—like how to store and use your sourdough discard—and then move on to different meal categories. Here's how it's laid out:

- **Breakfast & Brunch**: Start your day with wholesome, energy-boosting recipes like sourdough pancakes, muffins, and waffles.
- **Bread & Baked Goods:** Master the art of using discard in loaves of bread, pizza crusts, and biscuits.
- **Savory Snacks & Appetizers:** Find recipes for crackers, flatbreads, and other tasty snacks that will satisfy your cravings.
- **Lunch & Dinner Favorites**: Learn how to incorporate sourdough discard into hearty meals like veggie burgers, pot pies, and savory casseroles.
- **Desserts & Sweet Treats**: Yes, you can use sourdough discard in desserts! Get ready for cakes, cookies, and brownies with a tangy twist.
- **Gluten-Free Options**: A section dedicated to gluten-free recipes that still pack a punch in flavor and texture.

Each recipe is written in clear, straightforward steps so that anyone—whether you're a beginner or a seasoned home cook—can follow along with ease.

Meet Your 8 Exclusive Bonuses

To make your sourdough journey even more enjoyable, I've included eight exclusive bonuses designed to keep you organized, inspired, and committed to zero-waste cooking in your kitchen. These resources will help you make the most of your sourdough discard while enhancing your culinary experience.

1. **28-Day Zero-Waste Meal Plan:** Struggling to come up with new meal ideas? This 28-day plan provides you with a full month of zero-waste recipes, helping you reduce food waste while enjoying delicious meals.

2. **FAQ Guide:** Have questions about sourdough discard? This comprehensive guide covers the most frequently asked questions, offering solutions to common issues, so you can bake with confidence.

3. **Grocery Shopping Organizer Template:** Plan your grocery trips more efficiently with this organizer template, ensuring you buy exactly what you need for each recipe, reducing both waste and stress.

4. **Weekly Meal Planner:** Stay organized and reduce food waste by planning your weekly meals with ease. This planner helps you map out breakfast, lunch, and dinner for the week ahead.

5. **Alaska Sourdough Recipes:** Dive into the rich history of Alaska's sourdough traditions with this collection of hearty, time-honored recipes, perfect for the adventurous baker.

6. **Sourdough Traditions Around the World Recipes:** Explore sourdough recipes from different cultures, with unique flavors and techniques from around the globe.

7. **Starter Sourdough and Preservation Guide:** Learn how to create, maintain, and preserve your sourdough starter with this detailed guide. You'll master the art of sourdough, ensuring you always have a healthy starter on hand.

8. **Sweet Sourdough Baking Recipes:** Indulge your sweet tooth with this collection of sweet sourdough recipes, including cakes, pastries, and more, all made with your sourdough discard.

These bonuses are designed to complement the recipes in this book, giving you all the tools you need to build better habits in the kitchen. By the time you're finished, you'll not only master sourdough discard recipes but also feel more organized and confident in planning meals that support both your family and the environment.

Your Sourdough Journey Starts Here

Let's be honest—there's something deeply satisfying about making delicious food from scratch, especially when it involves ingredients that would otherwise go to waste. This cookbook isn't just about recipes; it's about embracing a mindset that values sustainability, creativity, and care in the kitchen.

By the end of this book, you'll not only have a collection of incredible dishes to share with your family and friends, but you'll also have a new perspective on how to use everything in your kitchen to its fullest potential. So, grab your sourdough starter, set your oven to preheat, and let's get cooking!

Chapter 2: Sourdough Discard Basics

Before we jump into the recipes, it's important to understand the star ingredient of this cookbook: sourdough discard. Knowing what it is, how to handle it, and why it's so valuable will set you up for success in the kitchen. So, let's take a closer look at this unassuming byproduct and discover how it can elevate your cooking.

What is Sourdough Discard?

If you're new to sourdough baking, the concept of discard might seem confusing. Here's the short version: every time you feed your sourdough starter (a mixture of flour and water that captures wild yeast and bacteria), you remove a portion of it to keep the balance of yeast and bacteria in check. This removed portion is what we call "discard."

But here's the key: discard isn't waste. It's still packed with flavor and active cultures, and while it may not have enough power to raise a loaf of bread, it's perfect for adding richness, depth, and a unique tang to other dishes. It's the secret ingredient that turns ordinary pancakes, muffins, or even pizza crust into something exceptional.

Why is Sourdough Discard So Special?

What makes sourdough discard different from regular flour? It's all in the fermentation. Sourdough discard has been through a natural fermentation process, which gives it that slight sourness and depth of flavor. This fermentation breaks down some of the complex carbohydrates in the flour, making it easier to digest and adding a nutritional boost to whatever you're cooking. You'll notice that recipes using discard have a distinctive tang, a rich texture, and an added complexity that's hard to replicate with other ingredients.

This means that when you use sourdough discard, you're not just adding flavor—you're adding character. It can take a simple recipe and give it a little extra something that makes it stand out.

How to Store and Preserve Your Sourdough Discard

Now that you know how amazing sourdough discard is, let's talk about how to store it. You'll be creating discard every time you feed your starter, and if you're not baking every day, you'll need to keep it fresh until you're ready to use it.

Here are the best ways to store and preserve your discard:

In the Refrigerator

The easiest and most common way to store sourdough discard is to keep it in the fridge. Simply transfer it to an airtight container, and it will stay fresh for up to a week. If you bake regularly, you can keep adding new discard to the same container, but be sure to use the oldest discard first to prevent spoilage.

Freezing for Later Use

Freezing is an excellent choice if you won't be using your waste straight soon. Portion it out into small amounts (like tablespoons or cups) and freeze it in ice cube trays or freezer-safe bags. When you're ready to bake, just thaw it in the fridge overnight or at room temperature for a few hours. Frozen discard can last for several months, making it a convenient option for when you need it on the fly.

Room Temperature for Immediate Use

If you're planning to use your discard within a day, you can leave it out at room temperature. This is great for when you want to bake later in the day or the next morning. Just remember to cover it loosely to allow some airflow while keeping it protected from dust or pests.

Drying Your Discard for Long-Term Storage

For those who want to store discard for even longer periods, drying it is an option. Spread a thin layer of discard onto a sheet of parchment paper and let it air-dry completely. Once dry, you can break it into pieces and store it in an airtight container. This method allows you to preserve discard for months, and when you're ready to use it, simply rehydrate it with equal parts water.

By storing your discard properly, you'll always have a supply ready to use in your recipes. And remember: discard is still "alive" with natural yeast, so treat it with care!

How to Tell If Your Discard Has Gone Bad

Although sourdough discard can last a while when stored correctly, it's important to know when it's time to toss it. Here are a few signs that your discard may have gone bad:

- **Smells off**: While sourdough discard naturally has a slightly tangy smell, if it starts to smell overly sour, like vinegar or alcohol, it's past its prime.

- **Mold or discoloration**: If you see any mold or strange colors (like pink or orange), it's time to throw it away.

- **Strange texture**: If your discard has separated into liquid and solids, with a strange texture, it's best not to use it. Some separation is normal (a layer of liquid on top called "hooch"), but if it looks slimy or chunky in an odd way, discard it.

Don't worry, though—if you're regularly using and refreshing your discard, it'll stay fresh and ready for all the recipes in this book.

Understanding the Different Types of Sourdough Discard

Not all sourdough discard is created equal. Depending on how long it's been sitting or how frequently you bake, your discard may have slightly different properties. Here's a quick breakdown of the types of discard you might encounter and how to use them:

Fresh Discard

Fresh discard comes straight from a recently fed starter. It's active, full of bubbles, and ready to use in recipes that don't require long fermentation. This is ideal for quick recipes like pancakes, muffins, or even pizza dough.

Older Discard

If your discard has been sitting in the fridge for a few days, it will still be perfectly fine to use, but it may have a more pronounced tangy flavor. This can be great for recipes where you want a stronger sourdough taste, like crackers or flatbreads.

Very Old Discard

If your discard has been sitting for over a week or more, it will have a much more intense flavor and may not be as bubbly. This type of discard is best for recipes where you want to hide the sourness, like in chocolate cakes or brownies, where the sweetness can balance out the tang.

Essential Tools for Sourdough Discard Cooking

You don't need a fully equipped professional kitchen to get started with sourdough discard recipes. However, having a few key tools will make your cooking experience smoother and more enjoyable. Here's what you'll need:

- **Mixing Bowls**: A variety of sizes is helpful for mixing doughs, batters, and dry ingredients. Opt for sturdy, non-slip bowls for ease of use.

- **Whisks and Spatulas**: You'll need a good whisk for combining wet and dry ingredients, and a silicone spatula is perfect for scraping down bowls and folding ingredients together.

- **Dough Scraper**: This simple tool will quickly become your best friend when working with sticky doughs. It's perfect for cutting, shaping, and cleaning up doughy messes.

- **Digital Scale**: Accuracy matters when baking, especially when feeding your sourdough starter. A digital scale ensures your measurements are spot on.

- **Baking Sheets and Parchment Paper**: Essential for baking everything from crackers to cookies, and parchment paper helps prevent sticking while making clean-up a breeze.

- **Cast Iron Skillet or Griddle**: Perfect for sourdough pancakes or flatbreads, a cast iron skillet provides even heating and a wonderful crust.

- **Loaf Pans and Muffin Tins**: For bread loaves, muffins, or even mini quiches, having a couple of these pans on hand will give you plenty of versatility.

Tips for Reducing Kitchen Waste

This book is not just about sourdough discard; it's about embracing a zero-waste philosophy in your kitchen. Here are a few simple ways to reduce waste while cooking:

1. **Repurpose Ingredients**: Got vegetable scraps? Use them to make stock. Leftover rice? Turn it into fried rice or rice pudding. Always look for ways to reuse ingredients.

2. **Compost**: Not everything can be reused, but instead of tossing food scraps into the trash, consider starting a compost bin. It's great for the environment and will give your garden a boost.

3. **Plan Your Meals**: One of the best ways to reduce waste is to plan ahead. Use the weekly meal planner included in this book to organize your meals, shop smart, and avoid buying more than you need.

4. **Store Smart**: Learning how to properly store food can make a huge difference in reducing waste. Keep your ingredients fresh for longer with airtight containers, and freeze leftovers for future meals.

I've created a weekly meal planner template just for you! Simply scan the QR code on the right to download and print it.:

Chapter 3: Breakfast & Brunch

1. Fluffy Sourdough Pancakes

👥 4 | ⏱ 10 min | 🍲 15 min

These pancakes are light, fluffy, and perfect for lazy weekend mornings. The tang from the sourdough discard adds a special twist to this breakfast staple.

Ingredients:

- 1 cup sourdough discard
- 1 cup all-purpose flour
- 1 cup milk
- 1 large egg, beaten
- 2 tablespoons melted butter
- 2 tablespoons sugar
- 1 teaspoon baking powder
- 1/2 teaspoon baking soda
- 1/2 teaspoon salt
- Butter or oil for cooking

Instructions:

1. In a large bowl, whisk together the sourdough discard, milk, egg, and melted butter.
2. In another bowl, combine the flour, sugar, baking powder, baking soda, and salt.
3. Gradually add the dry ingredients to the wet ingredients, stirring until just combined. Don't overmix!
4. Heat a skillet over medium heat and lightly grease with butter or oil.
5. Pour about 1/4 cup of batter onto the skillet for each pancake. Cook until bubbles form on the surface, about 2-3 minutes. Flip and cook until golden on the other side.
6. Serve warm with maple syrup or your favorite toppings.

2. Banana Sourdough Muffins

👥 12 muffins | ⏱ 10 min | 🍲 25 min

Perfect for using up ripe bananas and sourdough discard, these moist muffins are a hit with both kids and adults alike.

Ingredients:

- 1 cup sourdough discard
- 3 ripe bananas, mashed
- 1/2 cup vegetable oil
- 1/2 cup sugar
- 2 large eggs
- 1 teaspoon vanilla extract
- 1 teaspoon baking soda
- 1/2 teaspoon salt
- 1 1/2 cups all-purpose flour
- 1/2 cup chopped walnuts or chocolate chips (optional)

Instructions:

1. Preheat the oven to 350°F (175°C) and line a muffin tin with paper liners.
2. In a large bowl, mix the mashed bananas, sourdough discard, oil, sugar, eggs, and vanilla.
3. In a separate bowl, whisk together the flour, baking soda, and salt.
4. Add the dry ingredients to the wet mixture and stir until just combined. Fold in the walnuts or chocolate chips if using.
5. Divide the batter among the muffin cups, filling them about 2/3 full.
6. Bake for 20-25 minutes, or until a toothpick comes out clean. Cool on a wire rack.

3. Sourdough Waffles

👥 4 | ⏱ 10 min | 🍽 15 min

These waffles are golden and crispy on the outside, soft and tender on the inside. Perfect for any brunch, especially when topped with fresh fruit and whipped cream.

Ingredients:

- 1 cup sourdough discard
- 1 1/2 cups all-purpose flour
- 1 cup milk
- 1/4 cup vegetable oil
- 1 large egg
- 2 tablespoons sugar
- 1 teaspoon baking powder
- 1/2 teaspoon baking soda
- 1/4 teaspoon salt
- 1 teaspoon vanilla extract

Instructions:

1. In a large bowl, whisk together the sourdough discard, milk, egg, oil, and vanilla.
2. In another bowl, combine the flour, sugar, baking powder, baking soda, and salt.
3. Add the dry ingredients to the wet mixture, stirring until just combined.
4. Preheat your waffle iron and lightly grease it.
5. Pour the batter into the waffle iron and cook according to your waffle iron's instructions.
6. Serve warm with syrup, fresh fruit, or any toppings of your choice.

4. Morning Glory Sourdough Muffins

👥 12 muffins | ⏱ 15 min | 🍽 25 min

Packed with carrots, apples, and nuts, these muffins are wholesome and filling, perfect for a nutritious breakfast on the go.

Ingredients:

- 1 cup sourdough discard
- 1 1/2 cups all-purpose flour
- 1/2 cup sugar
- 1/2 cup vegetable oil
- 2 large eggs
- 1 teaspoon vanilla extract
- 1 teaspoon baking soda
- 1 teaspoon cinnamon
- 1/2 teaspoon salt
- 1 cup grated carrots
- 1 apple, peeled and grated
- 1/2 cup raisins
- 1/2 cup chopped walnuts or pecans

Instructions:

1. Preheat the oven to 350°F (175°C) and line a muffin tin with paper liners.
2. In a large bowl, mix the sourdough discard, oil, sugar, eggs, and vanilla.
3. In another bowl, whisk together the flour, baking soda, cinnamon, and salt.
4. Gradually add the dry ingredients to the wet mixture and stir until just combined.
5. Fold in the grated carrots, apple, raisins, and nuts.
6. Divide the batter among the muffin cups, filling each about 2/3 full.
7. Bake for 20-25 minutes, or until a toothpick comes out clean.

5. Cinnamon Sourdough Rolls

👥 12 rolls | ⏱ 30 min | 🍽 25 min

These rolls are soft, gooey, and filled with sweet cinnamon goodness. The sourdough discard adds depth to the dough, making these rolls irresistible.

Ingredients:

- 1 cup sourdough discard
- 3 cups all-purpose flour
- 1/2 cup warm milk
- 1/4 cup sugar

- 1/4 cup unsalted butter, melted
- 1 large egg
- 1 teaspoon vanilla extract
- 2 teaspoons instant yeast
- 1/2 teaspoon salt

For the Filling:

- 1/4 cup unsalted butter, softened
- 1/2 cup brown sugar
- 2 tablespoons cinnamon

Instructions:

1. In a large bowl, combine the sourdough discard, flour, milk, sugar, melted butter, egg, vanilla, yeast, and salt. Stir until a soft dough forms.
2. Knead the dough on a floured surface for about 5 minutes until smooth and elastic.
3. Let the dough rise in a greased bowl for 1-2 hours until doubled in size.
4. Roll the dough into a rectangle, spread with softened butter, and sprinkle with cinnamon sugar.
5. Roll tightly and slice into 12 rolls. Place in a greased baking dish and let rise for another 45 minutes.
6. Bake at 350°F (175°C) for 20-25 minutes.

6. Sourdough Crepes

👥 4 | ⏱ 10 min | 🍽 20 min

These thin, delicate crepes are perfect for a sweet or savory filling. The sourdough discard adds just the right amount of tang.

Ingredients:

- 1 cup sourdough discard
- 1 cup all-purpose flour
- 1 1/2 cups milk
- 2 large eggs
- 2 tablespoons melted butter
- 2 tablespoons sugar
- 1/4 teaspoon salt

Instructions:

1. In a large bowl, whisk together the sourdough discard, flour, milk, eggs, melted butter, sugar, and salt until smooth.
2. Heat a non-stick skillet over medium heat and lightly grease with butter.
3. Pour about 1/4 cup of batter into the skillet, swirling to spread it evenly.
4. Cook for 1-2 minutes, then flip and cook for another minute.
5. Serve with your favorite fillings like fruit, Nutella, or savory options like ham and cheese.

7. Sourdough Discard English Muffins

👥 8 muffins | ⏱ 15 min (+ overnight rest) | 🍽 10 min

Homemade English muffins are a game-changer. With sourdough discard, they have a unique tang that store-bought versions can't match.

Ingredients:

- 1 cup sourdough discard
- 3 cups all-purpose flour
- 1 tablespoon sugar
- 1 teaspoon salt
- 1 teaspoon baking soda
- 1 cup milk
- Cornmeal for dusting

Instructions:

1. The night before, mix sourdough discard with flour, sugar, and milk until smooth. Cover and let it rest overnight.
2. In the morning, gently incorporate salt and baking soda into the dough.
3. On a floured surface, roll out the dough to about 1/2 inch thick. Cut out rounds with a biscuit cutter.

4. Dust a baking sheet with cornmeal and place the muffins on it. Let them rise for about 45 minutes.
5. Heat a skillet over medium-low heat and cook the muffins for 5 minutes on each side, or until toasted.

8. Sourdough Breakfast Pizza

👥 4 | ⏱ 10 min | 🍲 15 min

A perfect breakfast twist on pizza! With a sourdough crust, topped with eggs, bacon, and cheese, it's an all-in-one breakfast dish.

Ingredients:

- 1 cup sourdough discard
- 1 1/2 cups all-purpose flour
- 1/2 teaspoon salt
- 1/4 teaspoon baking powder
- 1/2 cup water
- 1 tablespoon olive oil
- Toppings: scrambled eggs, bacon, cheese, veggies (as desired)

Instructions:

1. Preheat the oven to 425°F (220°C).
2. In a bowl, mix the sourdough discard, flour, salt, baking powder, water, and olive oil until a dough forms.
3. Roll out the dough on a floured surface and place it on a baking sheet.
4. Pre-bake the crust for 7-8 minutes.
5. Add scrambled eggs, bacon, cheese, and any other toppings you like. Bake for another 7-8 minutes until the cheese is melted and bubbly.

9. Sourdough Discard Bagels

👥 8 bagels | ⏱ 20 min (+ 1 hour rise) | 🍲 25 min

Homemade bagels made with sourdough discard are chewy, flavorful, and perfect for breakfast sandwiches.

Ingredients:

- 1 cup sourdough discard
- 3 cups all-purpose flour
- 1 tablespoon sugar
- 1 teaspoon salt
- 1 teaspoon instant yeast
- 1 cup warm water
- Sesame seeds, poppy seeds, or everything seasoning (optional)

Instructions:

1. In a large bowl, combine the sourdough discard, flour, sugar, salt, yeast, and warm water. Knead for 10 minutes until smooth.
2. Let the dough rise for 1 hour until doubled in size.
3. Divide the dough into 8 pieces and shape each into a bagel.
4. Boil the bagels in water for 1 minute on each side. Place them on a baking sheet and sprinkle with your desired toppings.
5. Bake at 425°F (220°C) for 20-25 minutes until golden.

10. Sourdough Discard Frittata

👥 6 | ⏱ 10 min | 🍲 20 min

This frittata, made with a sourdough crust, is perfect for brunch and can be filled with any veggies or proteins you have on hand.

Ingredients:

- 1 cup sourdough discard
- 1/4 cup all-purpose flour
- 1/2 teaspoon salt
- 4 large eggs
- 1/4 cup milk
- 1 cup spinach, chopped
- 1/2 cup mushrooms, sliced
- 1/2 cup shredded cheese

Instructions:

1. Preheat the oven to 350°F (175°C).

2. In a bowl, mix sourdough discard, flour, and salt. Pour into a greased pie dish.
3. In a separate bowl, whisk eggs and milk together. Stir in the spinach, mushrooms, and cheese.
4. Pour the egg mixture over the sourdough base and bake for 20-25 minutes until set.

11. Sourdough Discard Blueberry Pancakes

👥 4 | ⏱ 10 min | 🍲 15 min

Classic pancakes get a delicious upgrade with sourdough discard and fresh blueberries.

Ingredients:

- 1 cup sourdough discard
- 1 cup all-purpose flour
- 1 cup milk
- 1 large egg
- 2 tablespoons melted butter
- 1 tablespoon sugar
- 1 teaspoon baking powder
- 1/2 teaspoon salt
- 1/2 cup fresh or frozen blueberries

Instructions:

1. In a bowl, whisk together the sourdough discard, milk, egg, and melted butter.
2. In another bowl, combine the flour, sugar, baking powder, and salt.
3. Add the dry ingredients to the wet mixture and stir until just combined. Fold in the blueberries.
4. Heat a skillet and cook the pancakes, flipping when bubbles form.

12. Sourdough Discard Coffee Cake

👥 8 | ⏱ 15 min | 🍲 45 min

This sourdough coffee cake is moist, with a crumbly streusel topping, perfect for brunch or an afternoon treat.

Ingredients:

- 1 cup sourdough discard
- 1 1/2 cups all-purpose flour
- 1/2 cup sugar
- 1/2 cup melted butter
- 1 large egg
- 1 teaspoon vanilla extract
- 1 teaspoon baking powder
- 1/2 teaspoon salt

For the Streusel Topping:

- 1/2 cup brown sugar
- 1/4 cup flour
- 1/2 teaspoon cinnamon
- 1/4 cup melted butter

Instructions:

1. Preheat the oven to 350°F (175°C).
2. In a large bowl, mix the sourdough discard, sugar, melted butter, egg, and vanilla.
3. In another bowl, combine the flour, baking powder, and salt. Add to the wet ingredients and stir until combined.
4. Pour the batter into a greased 9-inch baking pan.
5. For the topping, mix all the streusel ingredients and sprinkle over the cake.
6. Bake for 45 minutes or until a toothpick comes out clean.

13. Sourdough Discard French Toast Bake

👥 6 | ⏱ 15 min | 🍽 30 min

This baked French toast is made with sourdough discard and leftover bread, perfect for using up extras and feeding a crowd.

Ingredients:

- 1 cup sourdough discard
- 6 slices of bread, cut into cubes
- 4 large eggs
- 1 1/2 cups milk
- 1/4 cup sugar
- 1 teaspoon vanilla extract
- 1/2 teaspoon cinnamon

Instructions:

1. Preheat the oven to 350°F (175°C) and grease a baking dish.
2. In a large bowl, whisk together the eggs, sourdough discard, milk, sugar, vanilla, and cinnamon.
3. Add the bread cubes to the mixture and stir to coat.
4. Pour the mixture into the prepared dish and bake for 25-30 minutes until golden and set.

14. Sourdough Discard Donuts

👥 12 donuts | ⏱ 15 min | 🍽 10 min

These baked donuts are soft, tender, and have just the right amount of tang from the sourdough discard.

Ingredients:

- 1 cup sourdough discard
- 2 cups all-purpose flour
- 1/2 cup sugar
- 1/4 cup melted butter
- 1/2 cup milk
- 1 large egg
- 1 teaspoon vanilla extract
- 1 teaspoon baking powder
- 1/2 teaspoon baking soda
- 1/2 teaspoon salt

Instructions:

1. Preheat the oven to 375°F (190°C) and grease a donut pan.
2. In a large bowl, mix the sourdough discard, flour, sugar, melted butter, milk, egg, and vanilla.
3. Stir in the baking powder, baking soda, and salt.
4. Spoon the batter into the donut pan and bake for 10-12 minutes until golden.
5. Let cool, then top with your favorite glaze or cinnamon sugar.

15. Sourdough Discard Granola

👥 8 | ⏱ 10 min | 🍽 30 min

Homemade granola made with sourdough discard is crunchy, slightly tangy, and perfect for topping yogurt or enjoying as a snack.

Ingredients:

- 1 cup sourdough discard
- 3 cups rolled oats
- 1/2 cup honey or maple syrup
- 1/4 cup melted coconut oil
- 1 teaspoon vanilla extract
- 1/2 teaspoon cinnamon
- 1/2 cup chopped nuts
- 1/4 cup dried fruit (optional)

Instructions:

1. Preheat the oven to 300°F (150°C) and line a baking sheet with parchment paper.
2. In a large bowl, mix the sourdough discard, oats, honey, coconut oil, vanilla, cinnamon, and nuts.
3. Spread the mixture evenly on the baking sheet and bake for 25-30 minutes, stirring halfway through.

4. Let cool, then stir in the dried fruit if using.

16. Sourdough Discard Scones

👥 8 | ⏱ 10 min | 🍲 20 min

These tender scones have a light tang from the sourdough discard and are perfect for serving with jam and clotted cream.

Ingredients:

- 1 cup sourdough discard
- 2 cups all-purpose flour
- 1/3 cup sugar
- 1 tablespoon baking powder
- 1/2 teaspoon salt
- 1/2 cup cold butter, cubed
- 1/4 cup heavy cream
- 1 teaspoon vanilla extract

Instructions:

1. Preheat the oven to 400°F (200°C).
2. In a large bowl, combine the flour, sugar, baking powder, and salt. Cut in the cold butter until the mixture resembles coarse crumbs.
3. Stir in the sourdough discard, heavy cream, and vanilla until just combined.
4. Turn the dough onto a floured surface, pat into a circle, and cut into 8 wedges.
5. Bake for 15-20 minutes until golden brown.

17. Sourdough Discard Omelette with Herbed Crust

👥 4 | ⏱ 10 min | 🍲 15 min

This omelette has a sourdough discard crust, giving it extra flavor and texture, perfect for a hearty breakfast.

Ingredients:

- 1 cup sourdough discard
- 4 large eggs
- 1/4 cup milk
- 1/4 cup chopped herbs (parsley, chives, basil)
- 1/2 cup shredded cheese
- Salt and pepper to taste

Instructions:

1. Preheat a non-stick skillet over medium heat.
2. Pour the sourdough discard into the skillet, spreading it out evenly.
3. In a bowl, whisk together eggs, milk, herbs, salt, and pepper.
4. Pour the egg mixture over the sourdough discard and cook until set, about 10-12 minutes.
5. Sprinkle cheese on top and fold the omelette in half before serving.

18. Sourdough Discard Apple Cinnamon Loaf

👥 8 | ⏱ 10 min | 🍲 45 min

This moist apple cinnamon loaf has a tender crumb, thanks to the sourdough discard, and is perfect with a cup of tea.

Ingredients:

- 1 cup sourdough discard
- 1 1/2 cups all-purpose flour
- 1/2 cup sugar
- 1/4 cup melted butter
- 1/2 cup milk
- 2 large eggs
- 1 teaspoon vanilla extract
- 1 teaspoon baking soda
- 1 teaspoon cinnamon
- 2 apples, peeled and diced

Instructions:

1. Preheat the oven to 350°F (175°C) and grease a loaf pan.
2. In a large bowl, mix the sourdough discard, flour, sugar, melted butter, milk, eggs, and vanilla.

3. Stir in the baking soda, cinnamon, and diced apples.
4. Pour the batter into the loaf pan and bake for 40–45 minutes, or until a toothpick comes out clean.

19. Sourdough Discard Dutch Baby

👥 4 | ⏱ 5 min | 🥣 20 min

This Dutch baby is an impressive breakfast dish that's part pancake, part popover, with a slight tang from the sourdough discard.

Ingredients:

- 1 cup sourdough discard
- 3/4 cup all-purpose flour
- 1 cup milk
- 3 large eggs
- 2 tablespoons sugar
- 1 teaspoon vanilla extract
- 1/4 teaspoon salt
- 2 tablespoons butter

Instructions:

1. Preheat the oven to 425°F (220°C). Place a cast-iron skillet in the oven to heat.
2. In a blender, combine the sourdough discard, flour, milk, eggs, sugar, vanilla, and salt. Blend until smooth.
3. Carefully remove the skillet from the oven and add the butter, swirling to coat the pan.
4. Pour the batter into the hot skillet and bake for 18-20 minutes, or until puffed and golden.
5. Serve immediately with powdered sugar and lemon juice.

20. Sourdough Discard Pumpkin Spice Scones

👥 8 | ⏱ 15 min | 🥣 25 min

These seasonal scones are packed with warm spices and a hint of pumpkin, with the added complexity of sourdough discard.

Ingredients:

- 1 cup sourdough discard
- 2 cups all-purpose flour
- 1/3 cup sugar
- 1 tablespoon baking powder
- 1 teaspoon pumpkin pie spice
- 1/2 teaspoon salt
- 1/2 cup cold butter, cubed
- 1/2 cup pumpkin puree
- 1/4 cup heavy cream

Instructions:

1. Preheat the oven to 400°F (200°C).
2. In a large bowl, combine the flour, sugar, baking powder, pumpkin pie spice, and salt. Cut in the butter until it resembles coarse crumbs.
3. Stir in the sourdough discard, pumpkin puree, and heavy cream until just combined.
4. Pat the dough into a circle, cut into 8 wedges, and place on a baking sheet.
5. Bake for 20-25 minutes until golden brown.

21. Sourdough Discard Apple Pancakes

👥 4 | ⏱ 10 min | 🥣 10 min

Light, fluffy pancakes with a tangy hint from sourdough discard, paired with the sweetness of apples.

Ingredients:

- 1 cup sourdough discard

- 1 cup all-purpose flour
- 1 teaspoon baking powder
- 1/2 teaspoon cinnamon
- 1 large egg
- 1 cup milk
- 1 tablespoon sugar
- 1 small apple, diced
- Butter for cooking

Instructions:

1. In a bowl, mix the sourdough discard, flour, baking powder, cinnamon, egg, milk, and sugar until smooth.
2. Stir in the diced apple.
3. Heat butter in a skillet over medium heat. Pour batter into the skillet and cook for 2-3 minutes on each side until golden.
4. Serve with syrup or additional apple slices.

22. Sourdough Discard Granola Bars

👥 12 bars | ⏲ 10 min | 🍲 25 min

Homemade granola bars packed with oats, nuts, and a slight sourdough tang, perfect for an on-the-go breakfast.

Ingredients:

- 1 cup sourdough discard
- 2 cups rolled oats
- 1/4 cup honey
- 1/2 cup peanut butter
- 1/4 cup chopped almonds
- 1/4 cup chocolate chips
- 1/2 teaspoon cinnamon
- 1/4 teaspoon salt

Instructions:

1. Preheat the oven to 350°F (175°C) and line an 8x8-inch pan with parchment paper.
2. In a bowl, mix sourdough discard, oats, honey, peanut butter, almonds, chocolate chips, cinnamon, and salt.

3. Press the mixture into the pan and bake for 20-25 minutes until golden.
4. Let cool before cutting into bars.

23. Sourdough Discard Sweet Potato Hash

👥 4 | ⏲ 15 min | 🍲 20 min

A savory and hearty breakfast hash using sourdough discard to bind the sweet potatoes and veggies.

Ingredients:

- 1 cup sourdough discard
- 2 medium sweet potatoes, diced
- 1/2 onion, chopped
- 1 bell pepper, chopped
- 2 cloves garlic, minced
- 2 tablespoons olive oil
- 4 large eggs
- Salt and pepper to taste

Instructions:

1. Heat olive oil in a skillet and sauté onions, peppers, and garlic for 5 minutes.
2. Add the diced sweet potatoes and cook until softened, about 10 minutes.
3. Stir in the sourdough discard, cooking until the mixture is golden and crispy.
4. Fry the eggs in a separate pan and serve on top of the hash.

24. Sourdough Discard Chia Pudding

👥 4 | ⏲ 5 min (+ chilling) | 🍲 N/A

A nutritious and easy make-ahead breakfast with a slight sourdough tang.

Ingredients:

- 1 cup sourdough discard
- 2 cups almond milk
- 1/2 cup chia seeds

- 2 tablespoons maple syrup
- 1 teaspoon vanilla extract

Instructions:

1. In a bowl, whisk together sourdough discard, almond milk, chia seeds, maple syrup, and vanilla.
2. Let sit for 5 minutes, then stir again to prevent clumping.
3. Cover and refrigerate for at least 4 hours or overnight.
4. Serve topped with fresh fruit or nuts.

25. Sourdough Discard Spinach Feta Muffins

👥 12 muffins | ⏱ 10 min | 🍲 20 min

Savory muffins perfect for breakfast, made with sourdough discard, spinach, and feta.

Ingredients:

- 1 cup sourdough discard
- 1 1/2 cups all-purpose flour
- 1/2 cup crumbled feta cheese
- 1 cup fresh spinach, chopped
- 1/4 cup olive oil
- 2 large eggs
- 1 teaspoon baking powder
- 1/2 teaspoon salt

Instructions:

1. Preheat the oven to 375°F (190°C) and grease a muffin tin.
2. In a bowl, mix the sourdough discard, flour, feta, spinach, olive oil, eggs, baking powder, and salt.
3. Divide the batter evenly into the muffin cups and bake for 18-20 minutes.
4. Serve warm or at room temperature.

26. Sourdough Discard Breakfast Burritos

👥 4 | ⏱ 10 min | 🍲 15 min

Fluffy scrambled eggs with sourdough discard tortillas, perfect for a filling breakfast.

Ingredients:

- 1 cup sourdough discard
- 2 cups all-purpose flour
- 1/2 teaspoon salt
- 1/4 cup water
- 6 large eggs, scrambled
- 1/2 cup shredded cheese
- 1/4 cup salsa
- 1 avocado, sliced

Instructions:

1. Mix sourdough discard, flour, salt, and water to form a dough. Roll into small tortillas.
2. Cook the tortillas on a hot skillet for 1-2 minutes per side until golden.
3. Fill each tortilla with scrambled eggs, cheese, salsa, and avocado. Roll into burritos.

27. Sourdough Discard Oatmeal

👥 2 | ⏱ 5 min | 🍲 10 min

A warm and comforting breakfast, with oats cooked in sourdough discard for a tangy twist.

Ingredients:

- 1/2 cup sourdough discard
- 1/2 cup rolled oats
- 1 cup almond milk
- 1 tablespoon honey
- 1/2 teaspoon cinnamon
- Fresh fruit for topping

Instructions:

1. In a small pot, combine sourdough discard, oats, almond milk, honey, and cinnamon.
2. Bring to a simmer, stirring frequently, until thickened, about 10 minutes.
3. Serve topped with fresh fruit.

28. Sourdough Discard Waffles

👥 4 | ⏱ 10 min | 🍲 10 min

Crispy on the outside and fluffy inside, these waffles are perfect for using up sourdough discard.

Ingredients:

- 1 cup sourdough discard
- 1 cup all-purpose flour
- 1/2 teaspoon baking powder
- 1 tablespoon sugar
- 1 large egg
- 1 cup milk
- 1/4 cup melted butter

Instructions:

1. Preheat your waffle iron.
2. In a bowl, mix the sourdough discard, flour, baking powder, sugar, egg, milk, and melted butter until smooth.
3. Cook the batter in the waffle iron according to the manufacturer's instructions until golden and crispy.

29. Sourdough Discard Veggie Frittata

👥 4 | ⏱ 10 min | 🍲 20 min

A healthy and filling frittata with mixed vegetables and a touch of sourdough discard.

Ingredients:

- 1 cup sourdough discard
- 6 large eggs
- 1 cup mixed vegetables (bell peppers, onions, spinach)
- 1/2 cup shredded cheese
- 1 tablespoon olive oil
- Salt and pepper to taste

Instructions:

1. Preheat the oven to 375°F (190°C).
2. In a skillet, heat the olive oil and sauté the vegetables until softened.
3. In a bowl, whisk together the eggs, sourdough discard, salt, and pepper.
4. Pour the egg mixture over the vegetables and sprinkle with cheese.
5. Bake in the oven for 15-20 minutes until set.

30. Sourdough Discard Breakfast Skillet

👥 4 | ⏱ 15 min | 🍲 15 min

A hearty one-pan breakfast skillet with potatoes, eggs, and sourdough discard.

Ingredients:

- 1 cup sourdough discard
- 2 medium potatoes, diced
- 1/2 onion, chopped
- 4 large eggs
- 1/4 cup shredded cheese
- 1 tablespoon olive oil
- Salt and pepper to taste

Instructions:

1. Heat olive oil in a skillet and cook the potatoes and onions until golden and crispy.
2. Stir in the sourdough discard and cook until combined and slightly browned.
3. Make small wells in the mixture and crack the eggs into the wells. Cover and cook until the eggs are set.
4. Sprinkle with cheese and serve hot.

Chapter 4: Bread & Baked Goods

1. Classic Sourdough Discard Bread

👥 1 loaf | ⏱ 20 min (+ rise) | 🍽 40 min

This simple loaf is perfect for using up sourdough discard, giving you a soft crumb and crispy crust.

Ingredients:

- 1 cup sourdough discard
- 3 cups all-purpose flour
- 1 cup warm water
- 1 teaspoon instant yeast
- 1 tablespoon sugar
- 1 teaspoon salt

Instructions:

1. In a large bowl, combine the sourdough discard, flour, water, yeast, sugar, and salt. Stir until a dough forms.
2. Turn the dough out onto a floured surface and knead for 8-10 minutes until smooth and elastic.
3. Place the dough in a greased bowl, cover, and let rise for 1-2 hours until doubled in size.
4. Preheat the oven to 425°F (220°C).
5. Shape the dough into a loaf and place it in a greased loaf pan. Let rise again for 30 minutes.
6. Bake for 35-40 minutes until golden and hollow-sounding when tapped.
7. Let cool before slicing.

2. Rosemary and Olive Oil Focaccia

👥 8 | ⏱ 15 min (+ rise) | 🍽 25 min

This airy focaccia is fragrant with rosemary and olive oil, making it a perfect side for soups or salads.

Ingredients:

- 1 cup sourdough discard
- 3 cups all-purpose flour
- 1 cup warm water
- 2 tablespoons olive oil
- 1 teaspoon instant yeast
- 1 teaspoon salt
- Fresh rosemary sprigs
- Coarse salt for sprinkling

Instructions:

1. Mix the sourdough discard, flour, water, olive oil, yeast, and salt in a bowl until a dough forms.
2. Knead the dough for about 10 minutes until smooth.
3. Transfer the dough to a greased bowl, cover, and let it rise for 1 hour.
4. Preheat the oven to 400°F (200°C).
5. Press the dough into a greased baking sheet, dimple the surface with your fingers, drizzle with olive oil, and sprinkle with rosemary and coarse salt.
6. Bake for 20-25 minutes until golden.

3. Sourdough Bagels

👥 8 bagels | ⏱ 30 min (+ rise) | 🍽 25 min

Chewy and delicious, these homemade sourdough bagels are perfect with cream cheese or smoked salmon.

Ingredients:

- 1 cup sourdough discard
- 3 cups all-purpose flour
- 1 tablespoon sugar
- 1 teaspoon salt
- 1 teaspoon yeast
- 1 cup warm water
- Toppings (sesame seeds, poppy seeds, etc.)

Instructions:

1. Mix the discard, flour, sugar, salt, yeast, and water until a dough forms.
2. Knead for 8-10 minutes until smooth. Let rise for 1-2 hours.
3. Divide the dough into 8 pieces, shape into bagels, and let rise for 30 minutes.
4. Preheat the oven to 425°F (220°C).
5. Boil the bagels for 1 minute per side, then sprinkle with toppings and bake for 20-25 minutes.

4. Sourdough Discard Garlic Knots

👥 8 knots | ⏱ 15 min (+ rise) | 🍲 20 min

These buttery garlic knots are soft and chewy, making them a perfect side dish for pasta or soups.

Ingredients:

- 1 cup sourdough discard
- 2 1/2 cups all-purpose flour
- 1 cup warm water
- 1 teaspoon yeast
- 1 tablespoon olive oil
- 1 teaspoon salt
- 2 tablespoons melted butter
- 2 cloves garlic, minced
- Fresh parsley for garnish

Instructions:

1. In a bowl, mix sourdough discard, flour, water, yeast, olive oil, and salt until a dough forms.
2. Knead for 5-7 minutes and let rise for 1-2 hours.
3. Divide the dough into 8 pieces, roll into ropes, and tie each rope into a knot.
4. Let rise for another 30 minutes while preheating the oven to 375°F (190°C).
5. Bake for 18-20 minutes.
6. Brush with melted butter mixed with garlic and sprinkle with parsley.

5. Cheddar Jalapeño Sourdough Bread

👥 1 loaf | ⏱ 20 min (+ rise) | 🍲 40 min

This cheesy, spicy sourdough bread is great for grilled cheese sandwiches or served alongside chili.

Ingredients:

- 1 cup sourdough discard
- 3 cups all-purpose flour
- 1 cup warm water
- 1 teaspoon yeast
- 1 tablespoon sugar
- 1 teaspoon salt
- 1 cup shredded cheddar cheese
- 1-2 jalapeños, diced

Instructions:

1. Combine the sourdough discard, flour, water, yeast, sugar, and salt. Knead for 8-10 minutes until smooth.
2. Add in the cheddar and jalapeños and knead until evenly distributed.
3. Let rise in a greased bowl for 1-2 hours.
4. Preheat the oven to 425°F (220°C).
5. Shape into a loaf, place in a greased loaf pan, and let rise for another 30 minutes.

6. Bake for 35-40 minutes until golden brown.

6. Sourdough Discard Pretzels

👥 **8 pretzels** | ⏱ **15 min (+ rise)** | 🍲 **15 min**

Soft, salty, and delicious, these pretzels are a fun way to use up sourdough discard and make a great snack or appetizer.

Ingredients:

- 1 cup sourdough discard
- 2 1/2 cups all-purpose flour
- 1 tablespoon sugar
- 1 teaspoon salt
- 1 teaspoon instant yeast
- 1 cup warm water
- Coarse salt for topping

Instructions:

1. Mix discard, flour, sugar, salt, yeast, and water into a dough and knead for 8-10 minutes.
2. Let rise for 1 hour. Preheat the oven to 450°F (230°C).
3. Divide the dough into 8 pieces and shape into pretzels.
4. Boil each pretzel for 1 minute, place on a baking sheet, and sprinkle with coarse salt.
5. Bake for 12-15 minutes until golden.

7. Sourdough Discard Flatbread

👥 **4** | ⏱ **10 min** | 🍲 **10 min**

This quick and easy flatbread is perfect for serving with dips or using as a pizza base.

Ingredients:

- 1 cup sourdough discard
- 1 1/2 cups all-purpose flour

- 1/2 teaspoon salt
- 1/2 teaspoon baking powder
- 1/4 cup water
- 2 tablespoons olive oil

Instructions:

1. Mix sourdough discard, flour, salt, baking powder, water, and olive oil until a dough forms.
2. Divide the dough into 4 pieces and roll each into a flat round.
3. Cook in a hot skillet for 2-3 minutes on each side until golden.
4. Serve warm with dips or top with your favorite pizza toppings.

8. Sourdough Discard Crackers

👥 **4** | ⏱ **10 min** | 🍲 **20 min**

Crispy and flavorful, these sourdough crackers are perfect for snacking or serving with cheese.

Ingredients:

- 1 cup sourdough discard
- 1 cup whole wheat flour
- 1 tablespoon olive oil
- 1/2 teaspoon salt
- 1 teaspoon dried herbs (optional)

Instructions:

1. Preheat the oven to 350°F (175°C).
2. Mix sourdough discard, flour, olive oil, salt, and herbs into a dough.
3. Roll out the dough thinly on a floured surface.
4. Cut into squares or desired shapes and place on a parchment-lined baking sheet.
5. Bake for 15-20 minutes until golden and crispy.

9. Sourdough Discard Breadsticks

👥 8 breadsticks | ⏱ 15 min (+ rise) | 🍲 20 min

These crispy, chewy breadsticks are perfect for dipping in marinara or enjoying as a snack.

Ingredients:

- 1 cup sourdough discard
- 2 1/2 cups all-purpose flour
- 1 teaspoon salt
- 1 tablespoon olive oil
- 1 teaspoon instant yeast
- 1/2 teaspoon sugar
- 1 cup warm water
- Parmesan cheese (optional)

Instructions:

1. Mix the sourdough discard, flour, salt, olive oil, yeast, sugar, and water into a dough. Knead for 8 minutes.
2. Let rise for 1 hour.
3. Preheat the oven to 375°F (190°C).
4. Roll the dough into breadstick shapes, sprinkle with Parmesan if desired, and bake for 15-20 minutes.

10. Sourdough Discard Pizza Dough

👥 4 | ⏱ 10 min (+ rise) | 🍲 15 min

This easy sourdough pizza dough has a crispy, chewy crust and can be topped with any ingredients you like.

Ingredients:

- 1 cup sourdough discard
- 2 1/2 cups all-purpose flour
- 1 cup warm water
- 1 teaspoon instant yeast
- 1 tablespoon olive oil
- 1 teaspoon salt

Instructions:

1. Mix the discard, flour, water, yeast, olive oil, and salt into a dough and knead for 10 minutes.
2. Let rise for 1 hour.
3. Preheat the oven to 450°F (230°C).
4. Roll out the dough on a floured surface and transfer to a pizza stone or baking sheet.
5. Add your favorite toppings and bake for 12-15 minutes.

11. Sourdough Discard Cheesy Biscuits

👥 8 biscuits | ⏱ 10 min | 🍲 15 min

These flaky, buttery biscuits are packed with cheesy goodness and are perfect alongside soup or chili.

Ingredients:

- 1 cup sourdough discard
- 2 cups all-purpose flour
- 1 tablespoon baking powder
- 1/2 teaspoon salt
- 1/2 cup cold butter, cubed
- 1 cup shredded cheddar cheese
- 1/2 cup milk

Instructions:

1. Preheat the oven to 400°F (200°C).
2. Mix the sourdough discard, flour, baking powder, and salt. Cut in the cold butter until the mixture resembles coarse crumbs.
3. Stir in the cheddar cheese and milk until just combined.
4. Drop spoonfuls of dough onto a baking sheet and bake for 12-15 minutes until golden.

12. Sourdough Discard Cinnamon Raisin Bread

👥 **1 loaf** | ⏱ **15 min (+ rise)** | 🍲 **40 min**

This sweet, cinnamon-swirled bread is studded with plump raisins and is perfect for toasting or making French toast.

Ingredients:

- 1 cup sourdough discard
- 3 cups all-purpose flour
- 1 cup warm water
- 1/2 cup sugar
- 1 teaspoon yeast
- 1 teaspoon salt
- 1/2 cup raisins
- 1 tablespoon cinnamon

Instructions:

1. Mix the discard, flour, water, sugar, yeast, and salt into a dough and knead for 8-10 minutes.
2. Add the raisins and cinnamon, kneading until well combined.
3. Let rise for 1 hour.
4. Preheat the oven to 375°F (190°C).
5. Shape into a loaf, place in a greased loaf pan, and let rise for another 30 minutes.
6. Bake for 35-40 minutes.

13. Sourdough Discard Cornbread

👥 **8** | ⏱ **10 min** | 🍲 **25 min**

This tangy, tender cornbread is perfect as a side for barbecue or chili.

Ingredients:

- 1 cup sourdough discard
- 1 cup cornmeal
- 1 cup all-purpose flour
- 1/4 cup sugar
- 1 tablespoon baking powder
- 1/2 teaspoon salt
- 1 cup milk
- 1/4 cup melted butter
- 1 large egg

Instructions:

1. Preheat the oven to 375°F (190°C).
2. In a large bowl, mix the sourdough discard, cornmeal, flour, sugar, baking powder, and salt.
3. Stir in the milk, melted butter, and egg until just combined.
4. Pour the batter into a greased 9x9-inch baking pan and bake for 25 minutes until golden.

14. Sourdough Discard Baguettes

👥 **2 baguettes** | ⏱ **15 min (+ rise)** | 🍲 **30 min**

These crusty, chewy baguettes are perfect for sandwiches or dipping in olive oil.

Ingredients:

- 1 cup sourdough discard
- 3 cups all-purpose flour
- 1 cup warm water
- 1 teaspoon yeast
- 1 tablespoon olive oil
- 1 teaspoon salt

Instructions:

1. Mix the discard, flour, water, yeast, olive oil, and salt into a dough and knead for 10 minutes.
2. Let rise for 1 hour.
3. Preheat the oven to 450°F (230°C).
4. Shape the dough into two baguettes and let rise for another 30 minutes.
5. Bake for 25-30 minutes until golden.

15. Sourdough Discard Brioche Buns

👥 8 buns | ⏱ 20 min (+ rise) | 🍽 20 min

These soft, buttery brioche buns are perfect for burgers or sandwiches.

Ingredients:

- 1 cup sourdough discard
- 3 cups all-purpose flour
- 1/2 cup warm milk
- 1/4 cup sugar
- 1/4 cup melted butter
- 2 large eggs
- 1 teaspoon yeast
- 1/2 teaspoon salt

Instructions:

1. Mix discard, flour, milk, sugar, melted butter, eggs, yeast, and salt into a dough.
2. Knead for 8-10 minutes until smooth. Let rise for 1-2 hours.
3. Divide the dough into 8 pieces, shape into buns, and let rise for another 30 minutes.
4. Preheat the oven to 375°F (190°C).
5. Bake for 18-20 minutes until golden brown.

16. Sourdough Discard Pita Bread

👥 6 | ⏱ 10 min (+ rise) | 🍽 10 min

This fluffy pita bread is perfect for stuffing with your favorite fillings or serving with dips.

Ingredients:

- 1 cup sourdough discard
- 2 1/2 cups all-purpose flour
- 1 teaspoon yeast
- 1/2 teaspoon salt
- 1 cup warm water

Instructions:

1. Mix the discard, flour, yeast, salt, and water into a dough and knead for 10 minutes.
2. Let rise for 1 hour.
3. Preheat the oven to 500°F (260°C).
4. Divide the dough into 6 pieces and roll each into a flat circle.
5. Bake directly on a baking stone or tray for 5-7 minutes until puffed.

17. Sourdough Discard Pizza Rolls

👥 12 rolls | ⏱ 15 min (+ rise) | 🍽 25 min

These cheesy, pepperoni-stuffed pizza rolls are great for parties or snacks.

Ingredients:

- 1 cup sourdough discard
- 2 1/2 cups all-purpose flour
- 1 teaspoon yeast
- 1 teaspoon sugar
- 1/2 teaspoon salt
- 1/2 cup warm water
- 1 cup shredded mozzarella
- 1/2 cup pepperoni slices

Instructions:

1. Mix the discard, flour, yeast, sugar, salt, and water into a dough and knead for 10 minutes.
2. Let rise for 1 hour.
3. Preheat the oven to 375°F (190°C).
4. Roll out the dough, layer with cheese and pepperoni, and roll up like cinnamon rolls.
5. Cut into 12 pieces and bake for 20-25 minutes.

18. Sourdough Discard Garlic Parmesan Knots

👥 8 knots | ⏱ 15 min (+ rise) | 🍲 20 min

These soft, buttery knots are infused with garlic and Parmesan, making them perfect for dipping in marinara sauce.

Ingredients:

- 1 cup sourdough discard
- 2 1/2 cups all-purpose flour
- 1 teaspoon salt
- 1 teaspoon yeast
- 1 tablespoon olive oil
- 1/2 teaspoon sugar
- 1 cup warm water
- 2 tablespoons melted butter
- 2 cloves garlic, minced
- 1/4 cup grated Parmesan cheese

Instructions:

1. Mix the discard, flour, salt, yeast, sugar, water, and olive oil into a dough. Knead for 8 minutes.
2. Let rise for 1 hour.
3. Divide the dough into 8 pieces, roll into ropes, and tie into knots. Let rise for 30 minutes.
4. Preheat the oven to 375°F (190°C). Bake for 15-20 minutes.
5. Brush with melted butter mixed with garlic and sprinkle with Parmesan.

19. Sourdough Discard Monkey Bread

👥 8 | ⏱ 20 min (+ rise) | 🍲 30 min

This pull-apart monkey bread is sticky, sweet, and has a delightful sourdough tang.

Ingredients:

- 1 cup sourdough discard
- 2 1/2 cups all-purpose flour
- 1/2 cup sugar
- 1/2 teaspoon salt
- 1 teaspoon yeast
- 1/2 cup warm milk
- 1/4 cup melted butter
- 1 teaspoon cinnamon

Instructions:

1. Mix the discard, flour, sugar, salt, yeast, milk, and melted butter into a dough. Knead for 8 minutes.
2. Let rise for 1 hour.
3. Preheat the oven to 350°F (175°C).
4. Roll the dough into balls and toss in cinnamon sugar. Place in a greased bundt pan.
5. Bake for 30-35 minutes until golden.

20. Sourdough Discard Chocolate Babka

👥 1 loaf | ⏱ 25 min (+ rise) | 🍲 45 min

This rich, chocolate-filled babka has a soft crumb and a hint of tang from the sourdough discard.

Ingredients:

- 1 cup sourdough discard
- 3 cups all-purpose flour
- 1/2 cup warm milk
- 1/4 cup sugar
- 1/4 cup melted butter
- 1 large egg
- 1 teaspoon yeast
- 1/2 teaspoon salt
- 1/2 cup chocolate spread

Instructions:

1. Mix discard, flour, milk, sugar, butter, egg, yeast, and salt into a dough.
2. Knead for 8-10 minutes and let rise for 1-2 hours.

3. Roll out the dough, spread with chocolate, and roll up tightly. Slice the roll lengthwise and twist the two strands together.
4. Place in a greased loaf pan and let rise for another 30 minutes.
5. Preheat the oven to 350°F (175°C) and bake for 40-45 minutes.

21. Sourdough Discard Focaccia

👥 8 | ⏱ 15 min | 🍽 20 min

A fluffy, airy focaccia with sourdough discard, topped with olive oil and fresh herbs.

Ingredients:

- 1 cup sourdough discard
- 3 cups all-purpose flour
- 1 teaspoon salt
- 1 cup warm water
- 1 tablespoon olive oil
- 1 teaspoon instant yeast
- Fresh rosemary and sea salt for topping

Instructions:

1. In a large bowl, combine sourdough discard, flour, salt, warm water, olive oil, and yeast. Knead until smooth. Cover and let rise for 1-2 hours.
2. Preheat the oven to 400°F (200°C).
3. Transfer the dough to a greased baking sheet, stretching it out into a rectangle. Dimple the surface with your fingers and drizzle with olive oil. Sprinkle with rosemary and sea salt.
4. Bake for 20-25 minutes until golden and crisp.

22. Sourdough Discard Pretzels

👥 8 | ⏱ 20 min | 🍽 15 min

Soft, chewy pretzels with a tangy flavor from sourdough discard.

Ingredients:

- 1 cup sourdough discard
- 3 cups all-purpose flour
- 1 teaspoon salt
- 1 tablespoon sugar
- 1 teaspoon instant yeast
- 1 cup warm water
- 1/4 cup baking soda (for boiling)
- Coarse salt for sprinkling

Instructions:

1. In a bowl, mix sourdough discard, flour, salt, sugar, yeast, and warm water to form a dough. Knead until smooth. Let rise for 1 hour.
2. Preheat the oven to 425°F (220°C). Bring a pot of water to a boil and add the baking soda.
3. Divide the dough into 8 pieces and roll into ropes. Shape into pretzels.
4. Boil each pretzel for 30 seconds, then transfer to a baking sheet. Sprinkle with coarse salt.
5. Bake for 12-15 minutes until golden brown.

23. Sourdough Discard Bagels

👥 8 | ⏱ 20 min | 🍽 20 min

Chewy, golden bagels with a sourdough discard base, perfect for breakfast.

Ingredients:

- 1 cup sourdough discard
- 4 cups bread flour
- 2 teaspoons salt
- 1 tablespoon sugar
- 1 teaspoon instant yeast
- 1 1/4 cups warm water
- 1 tablespoon honey (for boiling)
- Toppings (sesame seeds, poppy seeds, etc.)

Instructions:

1. In a large bowl, combine sourdough discard, flour, salt, sugar, yeast, and warm water. Knead for 8-10 minutes until smooth. Let rise for 1 hour.
2. Preheat the oven to 425°F (220°C). Bring a large pot of water to a boil and add the honey.
3. Shape the dough into 8 balls, then poke a hole in the center to form bagels.
4. Boil the bagels for 1-2 minutes on each side, then transfer to a baking sheet. Add toppings.
5. Bake for 15-20 minutes until golden.

24. Sourdough Discard Garlic Knots

👥 8 | ⏱ 10 min | 🍽 15 min

Soft, buttery garlic knots made with sourdough discard, perfect as a side for pasta.

Ingredients:

- 1 cup sourdough discard
- 3 cups all-purpose flour
- 1 teaspoon salt
- 1 teaspoon sugar
- 1 teaspoon instant yeast
- 1 cup warm water
- 1/4 cup melted butter
- 2 cloves garlic, minced
- Fresh parsley for garnish

Instructions:

1. In a bowl, mix sourdough discard, flour, salt, sugar, yeast, and warm water. Knead until smooth and let rise for 1 hour.
2. Preheat the oven to 375°F (190°C).
3. Divide the dough into 8 pieces and roll each into a rope. Tie each rope into a knot.
4. Bake for 12-15 minutes until golden.

5. Toss the hot garlic knots in melted butter mixed with garlic and garnish with parsley.

25. Sourdough Discard Dinner Rolls

👥 12 rolls | ⏱ 15 min | 🍽 20 min

Soft, fluffy dinner rolls made with sourdough discard, perfect for any meal.

Ingredients:

- 1 cup sourdough discard
- 3 cups all-purpose flour
- 2 tablespoons sugar
- 1 teaspoon salt
- 1 tablespoon melted butter
- 1 teaspoon instant yeast
- 1 cup warm water

Instructions:

1. In a large bowl, mix sourdough discard, flour, sugar, salt, butter, yeast, and warm water. Knead until smooth. Let rise for 1-2 hours.
2. Preheat the oven to 375°F (190°C).
3. Divide the dough into 12 pieces and shape into balls. Place in a greased baking dish and let rise again for 30 minutes.
4. Bake for 15-20 minutes until golden brown.

26. Sourdough Discard Brioche

👥 8 | ⏱ 20 min | 🍽 35 min

A rich, buttery brioche loaf made with sourdough discard, perfect for breakfast or a sweet treat.

Ingredients:

- 1 cup sourdough discard
- 3 cups all-purpose flour
- 1/4 cup sugar
- 1/2 teaspoon salt
- 1/2 cup unsalted butter, softened

- 3 large eggs
- 1 teaspoon instant yeast
- 1/4 cup warm milk

Instructions:

1. In a bowl, mix sourdough discard, flour, sugar, salt, softened butter, eggs, yeast, and warm milk until a soft dough forms. Knead for 8-10 minutes until smooth. Let rise for 1-2 hours.
2. Preheat the oven to 350°F (175°C).
3. Shape the dough into a loaf and place in a greased loaf pan. Let rise for another 30 minutes.
4. Bake for 30-35 minutes until golden brown.

27. Sourdough Discard Pita Bread

👥 8 | ⏱ 10 min | 🍲 10 min

Soft and fluffy pita bread made with sourdough discard, ideal for sandwiches or dips.

Ingredients:

- 1 cup sourdough discard
- 2 1/2 cups all-purpose flour
- 1 teaspoon salt
- 1 teaspoon sugar
- 1 teaspoon instant yeast
- 3/4 cup warm water

Instructions:

1. In a large bowl, mix sourdough discard, flour, salt, sugar, yeast, and warm water until a dough forms. Knead for 5-7 minutes until smooth. Let rise for 1 hour.
2. Preheat a cast iron skillet or baking stone in the oven to 500°F (260°C).
3. Divide the dough into 8 pieces and roll each into a ball. Flatten each ball into a circle.

4. Bake on the hot skillet or stone for 3-4 minutes until puffed and golden.

28. Sourdough Discard Flatbread

👥 8 | ⏱ 10 min | 🍲 10 min

A quick, versatile flatbread made with sourdough discard, perfect for sandwiches or pizzas.

Ingredients:

- 1 cup sourdough discard
- 2 cups all-purpose flour
- 1/2 teaspoon salt
- 1/4 teaspoon baking powder
- 3/4 cup warm water
- Olive oil for cooking

Instructions:

1. In a bowl, mix sourdough discard, flour, salt, baking powder, and water until a dough forms.
2. Divide the dough into 8 pieces and roll each into a flat round.
3. Heat olive oil in a skillet over medium heat. Cook each flatbread for 2-3 minutes per side until golden.
4. Serve warm with your favorite toppings or dips.

29. Sourdough Discard Naan

👥 8 | ⏱ 15 min | 🍲 10 min

Soft, pillowy naan bread with a subtle sourdough flavor, perfect for curries and dips.

Ingredients:

- 1 cup sourdough discard
- 2 1/2 cups all-purpose flour
- 1/2 teaspoon salt
- 1 teaspoon sugar

- 1 teaspoon instant yeast
- 1/2 cup warm water
- 1/4 cup yogurt
- 1 tablespoon melted butter

Instructions:

1. In a large bowl, combine sourdough discard, flour, salt, sugar, yeast, water, yogurt, and melted butter. Knead until smooth. Let rise for 1 hour.
2. Divide the dough into 8 pieces and roll each into a flat circle.
3. Preheat a skillet over medium-high heat and cook each naan for 2-3 minutes per side, until bubbles form and golden spots appear.
4. Brush with melted butter and serve warm.

30. Sourdough Discard Crusty Artisan Bread

👥 8 | ⏱ 15 min | 🍲 40 min

A beautifully crusty and chewy artisan bread made with sourdough discard, perfect for any occasion.

Ingredients:

- 1 cup sourdough discard
- 3 1/2 cups all-purpose flour
- 1 1/2 teaspoons salt
- 1 1/4 cups warm water
- 1 teaspoon instant yeast

Instructions:

1. In a large bowl, combine sourdough discard, flour, salt, water, and yeast. Stir until a shaggy dough forms. Cover and let rise for 2-3 hours, or until doubled in size.
2. Preheat the oven to 450°F (230°C) and place a Dutch oven inside to heat up.
3. Shape the dough into a round loaf. Place it on a piece of parchment paper and carefully transfer it to the preheated Dutch oven.
4. Cover and bake for 25 minutes. Remove the lid and bake for another 15 minutes until golden and crusty.

Chapter 5: Savory Snacks & Appetizers

1. Sourdough Discard Soft Pretzel Bites

👥 4 | ⏱ 15 min (+ rise) | 🍲 12 min

These soft pretzel bites are perfect for dipping in mustard or cheese sauce. They're bite-sized and full of flavor.

Ingredients:

- 1 cup sourdough discard
- 2 1/2 cups all-purpose flour
- 1 teaspoon yeast
- 1/2 teaspoon sugar
- 1 teaspoon salt
- 1 cup warm water
- Coarse salt for topping

Instructions:

1. Mix sourdough discard, flour, yeast, sugar, salt, and warm water to form a dough. Knead for 8-10 minutes.
2. Let rise for 1 hour.
3. Preheat the oven to 425°F (220°C).
4. Roll the dough into ropes and cut into bite-sized pieces. Boil for 1 minute per side.
5. Place on a baking sheet, sprinkle with coarse salt, and bake for 12 minutes.

2. Sourdough Discard Cheese Crackers

👥 4 | ⏱ 10 min | 🍲 20 min

These cheesy crackers are crispy, tangy, and make the perfect snack or addition to a cheese board.

Ingredients:

- 1 cup sourdough discard
- 1 cup all-purpose flour
- 1 cup grated cheddar cheese
- 1/4 cup butter, cold and cubed
- 1/4 teaspoon salt
- 1/4 teaspoon garlic powder (optional)

Instructions:

1. Preheat the oven to 350°F (175°C).
2. Mix the sourdough discard, flour, cheese, butter, salt, and garlic powder until a dough forms.
3. Roll out the dough thinly and cut into squares.
4. Place on a parchment-lined baking sheet and bake for 15-20 minutes until crispy.

3. Sourdough Discard Zucchini Fritters

👥 4 | ⏱ 10 min | 🍲 10 min

These crispy zucchini fritters are a perfect appetizer or snack, with a hint of tang from the sourdough discard.

Ingredients:

- 1 cup sourdough discard
- 1 cup shredded zucchini
- 1/4 cup grated Parmesan
- 1 egg
- 1/4 cup all-purpose flour
- 1/2 teaspoon salt
- 1/4 teaspoon black pepper
- Olive oil for frying

Instructions:

1. In a large bowl, mix the sourdough discard, zucchini, Parmesan, egg, flour, salt, and pepper.
2. Heat a tablespoon of olive oil in a skillet over medium heat.

3. Drop spoonfuls of batter into the skillet and flatten slightly.
4. Fry for 2-3 minutes per side, until golden and crispy.
5. Drain on paper towels and serve warm.

4. Sourdough Discard Garlic Parmesan Breadsticks

👥 6 | ⏱ 10 min (+ rise) | 🍽 12 min

These crispy, chewy breadsticks are flavored with garlic and Parmesan, perfect for dipping in marinara or enjoying on their own.

Ingredients:

- 1 cup sourdough discard
- 2 cups all-purpose flour
- 1 teaspoon yeast
- 1 teaspoon sugar
- 1/2 teaspoon salt
- 1 tablespoon olive oil
- 1/4 cup grated Parmesan cheese
- 2 cloves garlic, minced

Instructions:

1. In a large bowl, combine the sourdough discard, flour, yeast, sugar, salt, and olive oil. Knead for 8-10 minutes.
2. Let rise for 1 hour.
3. Preheat the oven to 400°F (200°C).
4. Roll the dough into breadstick shapes, brush with olive oil, and sprinkle with Parmesan and garlic.
5. Bake for 12-15 minutes until golden.

5. Sourdough Discard Onion Rings

👥 4 | ⏱ 10 min | 🍽 10 min

These crispy onion rings have a light batter made with sourdough discard, giving them a subtle tang.

Ingredients:

- 1 cup sourdough discard
- 1/2 cup all-purpose flour
- 1/4 cup cornstarch
- 1 teaspoon baking powder
- 1/2 teaspoon salt
- 1/2 teaspoon paprika
- 1/2 cup sparkling water
- 2 large onions, sliced into rings
- Oil for frying

Instructions:

1. Heat oil in a large pot to 350°F (175°C).
2. In a bowl, mix the sourdough discard, flour, cornstarch, baking powder, salt, paprika, and sparkling water.
3. Dip the onion rings into the batter, shaking off the excess.
4. Fry for 2-3 minutes until golden and crispy.
5. Drain on paper towels and serve immediately.

6. Sourdough Discard Spinach Dip Bread Bowl

👥 6 | ⏱ 15 min | 🍽 30 min

This warm, creamy spinach dip is served in a hollowed-out sourdough discard bread bowl, making it a show-stopping appetizer.

Ingredients:

- 1 cup sourdough discard (for bread)
- 3 cups all-purpose flour
- 1 cup warm water
- 1 teaspoon yeast
- 1 teaspoon salt

For the Spinach Dip:

- 1 cup sour cream
- 1 cup cream cheese, softened
- 1 cup chopped spinach, cooked and drained
- 1/4 cup grated Parmesan

- 1/4 teaspoon garlic powder
- Salt and pepper to taste

Instructions:

1. Mix the sourdough discard, flour, water, yeast, and salt into a dough and knead for 10 minutes. Let rise for 1-2 hours.
2. Shape into a round loaf, let rise for another 30 minutes, then bake at 375°F (190°C) for 30 minutes.
3. Hollow out the center of the loaf to create a bread bowl.
4. In a separate bowl, mix the spinach dip ingredients until smooth.
5. Spoon the dip into the bread bowl and serve with the hollowed-out bread pieces for dipping.

7. Sourdough Discard Jalapeño Cheddar Poppers

👥 6 | ⏱ 10 min | 🍲 10 min

These spicy, cheesy jalapeño poppers have a light, tangy sourdough batter, perfect for parties or snacks.

Ingredients:

- 1 cup sourdough discard
- 1/2 cup all-purpose flour
- 1/4 cup cornstarch
- 1/2 teaspoon salt
- 1/2 cup milk
- 12 jalapeños, halved and seeded
- 1 cup shredded cheddar cheese
- Oil for frying

Instructions:

1. Heat oil to 350°F (175°C).
2. In a bowl, mix sourdough discard, flour, cornstarch, salt, and milk to create a batter.
3. Stuff each jalapeño half with cheddar cheese.

4. Dip the stuffed jalapeños in the batter and fry for 2-3 minutes until golden.
5. Drain on paper towels and serve.

8. Sourdough Discard Parmesan Crackers

👥 4 | ⏱ 10 min | 🍲 15 min

These thin, crispy crackers are packed with Parmesan and have a slight tang from the sourdough discard. Perfect for serving with dips or cheese.

Ingredients:

- 1 cup sourdough discard
- 1 cup all-purpose flour
- 1/4 cup grated Parmesan
- 1/4 cup butter, cold and cubed
- 1/2 teaspoon salt
- 1/4 teaspoon black pepper

Instructions:

1. Preheat the oven to 350°F (175°C).
2. Mix the sourdough discard, flour, Parmesan, butter, salt, and pepper until a dough forms.
3. Roll out the dough thinly and cut into shapes.
4. Place on a parchment-lined baking sheet and bake for 12-15 minutes until golden and crispy.

9. Sourdough Discard Stuffed Mushrooms

👥 4 | ⏱ 15 min | 🍲 20 min

These savory stuffed mushrooms are filled with a sourdough discard mixture that's cheesy, garlicky, and delicious.

Ingredients:

- 12 large mushrooms, stems removed
- 1/2 cup sourdough discard

- 1/4 cup breadcrumbs
- 1/4 cup grated Parmesan
- 1 clove garlic, minced
- 1 tablespoon olive oil
- Salt and pepper to taste

Instructions:

1. Preheat the oven to 375°F (190°C).
2. In a bowl, mix the sourdough discard, breadcrumbs, Parmesan, garlic, olive oil, salt, and pepper.
3. Stuff each mushroom cap with the mixture and place on a baking sheet.
4. Bake for 18-20 minutes until golden and bubbling.

10. Sourdough Discard Empanadas

👥 6 | ⏱ 20 min (+ rise) | 🍽 25 min

These flaky empanadas are filled with your favorite savory fillings, with a crust made from sourdough discard.

Ingredients:

- 1 cup sourdough discard
- 2 1/2 cups all-purpose flour
- 1 teaspoon salt
- 1/4 cup cold butter, cubed
- 1/4 cup cold water
- Your choice of filling (beef, chicken, cheese, etc.)

Instructions:

1. In a bowl, mix sourdough discard, flour, salt, butter, and water until a dough forms. Knead briefly.
2. Let the dough rest in the fridge for 30 minutes.
3. Preheat the oven to 375°F (190°C).
4. Roll out the dough and cut into circles. Add your desired filling to each circle and fold over, sealing the edges.
5. Bake for 20-25 minutes until golden.

11. Sourdough Discard Cornbread Muffins

👥 12 muffins | ⏱ 10 min | 🍽 25 min

These tangy cornbread muffins are light, fluffy, and perfect as a side for soups, chili, or barbecue.

Ingredients:

- 1 cup sourdough discard
- 1 cup cornmeal
- 1 cup all-purpose flour
- 1/4 cup sugar
- 1 tablespoon baking powder
- 1/2 teaspoon salt
- 1/4 cup melted butter
- 1 cup milk
- 1 large egg

Instructions:

1. Preheat the oven to 375°F (190°C) and line a muffin tin with paper liners.
2. In a bowl, mix the sourdough discard, cornmeal, flour, sugar, baking powder, and salt.
3. Stir in the melted butter, milk, and egg until just combined.
4. Divide the batter among the muffin cups and bake for 20-25 minutes until golden.

12. Sourdough Discard Puff Pastry Pinwheels

👥 12 pinwheels | ⏱ 15 min | 🍽 12 min

These flaky pinwheels are filled with a savory mixture of cheese and herbs, perfect for an appetizer or party snack.

Ingredients:

- 1 cup sourdough discard
- 1 1/2 cups all-purpose flour
- 1/2 cup cold butter, cubed
- 1/4 teaspoon salt

- 1/4 cup cold water
- 1/2 cup shredded cheese
- 2 tablespoons chopped herbs (thyme, rosemary, etc.)

Instructions:

1. In a bowl, mix the sourdough discard, flour, butter, salt, and water until a dough forms. Chill for 30 minutes.
2. Preheat the oven to 400°F (200°C).
3. Roll out the dough into a rectangle and sprinkle with cheese and herbs.
4. Roll up the dough and slice into pinwheels.
5. Bake for 10-12 minutes until golden and flaky.

13. Sourdough Discard Veggie Fritters

👥 4 | ⏱ 10 min | 🍲 10 min

These crispy veggie fritters are a great way to use up extra vegetables, with a light sourdough discard batter.

Ingredients:

- 1 cup sourdough discard
- 1 cup shredded zucchini or carrots
- 1/4 cup grated Parmesan
- 1 egg
- 1/4 cup all-purpose flour
- 1/4 teaspoon salt
- Olive oil for frying

Instructions:

1. In a large bowl, mix the sourdough discard, shredded veggies, Parmesan, egg, flour, and salt.
2. Heat a tablespoon of olive oil in a skillet over medium heat.
3. Drop spoonfuls of the batter into the skillet and flatten slightly.
4. Fry for 2-3 minutes per side until golden and crispy. Serve warm.

14. Sourdough Discard Mini Quiches

👥 12 mini quiches | ⏱ 10 min | 🍲 25 min

These mini quiches are baked in a sourdough crust and filled with your favorite savory ingredients, making them perfect for brunch or a snack.

Ingredients:

- 1 cup sourdough discard
- 1 1/2 cups all-purpose flour
- 1/4 cup cold butter, cubed
- 1/4 teaspoon salt
- 1/4 cup cold water
- 4 large eggs
- 1/2 cup milk
- 1/2 cup shredded cheese
- Your choice of filling (spinach, mushrooms, bacon, etc.)

Instructions:

1. Preheat the oven to 375°F (190°C) and grease a muffin tin.
2. Mix the sourdough discard, flour, butter, salt, and water until a dough forms. Chill for 15 minutes.
3. Roll out the dough and cut circles to fit in the muffin tin.
4. In a separate bowl, whisk together the eggs, milk, cheese, and fillings.
5. Pour the filling into the dough-lined muffin cups and bake for 20-25 minutes.

15. Sourdough Discard Mozzarella Sticks

👥 6 | ⏱ 15 min | 🍲 10 min

These crunchy mozzarella sticks are coated in a sourdough discard batter and fried to golden perfection.

Ingredients:

- 1 cup sourdough discard
- 1/2 cup all-purpose flour
- 1/4 cup cornstarch
- 1/2 teaspoon salt
- 1/2 cup milk
- 12 mozzarella sticks
- Oil for frying

Instructions:

1. Heat oil in a pot to 350°F (175°C).
2. In a bowl, mix the sourdough discard, flour, cornstarch, salt, and milk to create a batter.
3. Dip each mozzarella stick into the batter, then fry for 2-3 minutes until golden and crispy.
4. Drain on paper towels and serve immediately with marinara sauce.

16. Sourdough Discard Pizza Bites

👥 12 bites | ⏱ 10 min | 🍲 12 min

These bite-sized pizza rolls are stuffed with cheese and pepperoni, making them perfect for parties or snacks.

Ingredients:

- 1 cup sourdough discard
- 2 cups all-purpose flour
- 1 teaspoon yeast
- 1/2 teaspoon sugar
- 1/2 teaspoon salt
- 1/2 cup warm water
- 1 cup shredded mozzarella
- 1/4 cup mini pepperoni

Instructions:

1. Mix the discard, flour, yeast, sugar, salt, and water into a dough. Knead for 10 minutes.
2. Let rise for 1 hour.

3. Preheat the oven to 375°F (190°C).
4. Roll out the dough and cut into small circles. Fill each with cheese and pepperoni, then fold over to seal.
5. Bake for 10-12 minutes until golden.

17. Sourdough Discard Hummus Flatbread

👥 4 | ⏱ 10 min | 🍲 10 min

This soft flatbread is perfect for serving with hummus or other dips, and the sourdough discard adds a hint of tanginess.

Ingredients:

- 1 cup sourdough discard
- 1 1/2 cups all-purpose flour
- 1/4 teaspoon salt
- 1/2 teaspoon baking powder
- 1/2 cup water
- 1 tablespoon olive oil

Instructions:

1. Mix the sourdough discard, flour, salt, baking powder, water, and olive oil into a dough.
2. Divide the dough into 4 pieces and roll each into a flat circle.
3. Heat a skillet over medium heat and cook each flatbread for 2-3 minutes on each side until golden.
4. Serve with hummus or your favorite dips.

18. Sourdough Discard Spinach Artichoke Dip Bites

👥 6 | ⏱ 15 min | 🍲 15 min

These savory bites are filled with creamy spinach and artichoke dip, baked in a sourdough discard crust.

Ingredients:

- 1 cup sourdough discard

- 1 1/2 cups all-purpose flour
- 1/4 cup cold butter, cubed
- 1/4 teaspoon salt
- 1/4 cup cold water

For the Filling:

- 1/2 cup cream cheese, softened
- 1/2 cup spinach, cooked and drained
- 1/4 cup artichoke hearts, chopped
- 1/4 cup grated Parmesan

Instructions:

1. Preheat the oven to 375°F (190°C).
2. Mix the sourdough discard, flour, butter, salt, and water into a dough. Chill for 15 minutes.
3. Roll out the dough and cut into small circles. Place in a mini muffin tin.
4. In a separate bowl, mix the filling ingredients.
5. Spoon the filling into the dough cups and bake for 12-15 minutes.

19. Sourdough Discard Chicken Tenders

👥 4 | ⏱ 10 min | 🍲 12 min

These crispy chicken tenders are coated in a tangy sourdough discard batter and fried until golden.

Ingredients:

- 1 cup sourdough discard
- 1/2 cup all-purpose flour
- 1/4 cup cornstarch
- 1/2 teaspoon salt
- 1/4 teaspoon black pepper
- 1/2 cup milk
- 1 lb chicken tenders
- Oil for frying

Instructions:

1. Heat oil in a pot to 350°F (175°C).

2. In a bowl, mix sourdough discard, flour, cornstarch, salt, pepper, and milk to create a batter.
3. Dip each chicken tender into the batter, then fry for 10-12 minutes until golden and cooked through.
4. Drain on paper towels and serve with dipping sauce.

20. Sourdough Discard Sausage Rolls

👥 6 | ⏱ 15 min (+ rise) | 🍲 20 min

These flaky sausage rolls are wrapped in a sourdough discard dough, perfect for appetizers or snacks.

Ingredients:

- 1 cup sourdough discard
- 2 cups all-purpose flour
- 1/4 teaspoon salt
- 1/4 cup cold butter, cubed
- 1/4 cup cold water
- 6 sausage links

Instructions:

1. In a bowl, mix sourdough discard, flour, butter, salt, and water into a dough. Chill for 30 minutes.
2. Preheat the oven to 400°F (200°C).
3. Roll out the dough and wrap each sausage link. Place on a baking sheet and bake for 20 minutes until golden.

21. Sourdough Discard Cheese Straws

👥 12 | ⏱ 10 min | 🍲 15 min

Crispy, cheesy straws with a slight sourdough tang, perfect as a snack or party appetizer.

Ingredients:

- 1 cup sourdough discard

- 1 1/2 cups all-purpose flour
- 1/2 cup grated cheddar cheese
- 1/4 cup grated Parmesan cheese
- 1/2 teaspoon salt
- 1/2 teaspoon paprika
- 1/4 cup cold butter, cubed

Instructions:

1. Preheat the oven to 375°F (190°C) and line a baking sheet with parchment paper.
2. In a bowl, mix the sourdough discard, flour, cheeses, salt, paprika, and cold butter until crumbly.
3. Roll out the dough into a rectangle, cut into thin strips, and twist each strip.
4. Bake for 12-15 minutes until golden and crispy.

22. Sourdough Discard Spinach & Artichoke Dip

👥 6 | ⏱ 10 min | 🍽 20 min

A creamy, tangy spinach and artichoke dip with the addition of sourdough discard, served with crackers or bread.

Ingredients:

- 1/2 cup sourdough discard
- 1 cup chopped spinach (fresh or frozen)
- 1 cup chopped artichoke hearts
- 1/2 cup cream cheese
- 1/4 cup sour cream
- 1/4 cup grated Parmesan
- 1/2 teaspoon garlic powder
- Salt and pepper to taste

Instructions:

1. Preheat the oven to 375°F (190°C).
2. In a bowl, mix the sourdough discard, spinach, artichokes, cream cheese, sour cream, Parmesan, garlic powder, salt, and pepper.
3. Transfer to a baking dish and bake for 20 minutes until bubbly and golden.

4. Serve with crackers, pita bread, or sourdough toast..

23. Sourdough Discard Savory Crackers

👥 24 crackers | ⏱ 10 min | 🍽 15 min

Crispy, homemade crackers with a sourdough discard base, perfect for snacking or as an appetizer.

Ingredients:

- 1 cup sourdough discard
- 1 1/2 cups all-purpose flour
- 1/4 cup olive oil
- 1 teaspoon salt
- 1 teaspoon dried herbs (rosemary, thyme, etc.)

Instructions:

1. Preheat the oven to 350°F (175°C) and line a baking sheet with parchment paper.
2. In a bowl, mix the sourdough discard, flour, olive oil, salt, and herbs until a dough forms.
3. Roll out the dough thinly and cut into crackers.
4. Transfer to the baking sheet and bake for 12-15 minutes until golden and crisp.

24. Sourdough Discard Pesto Pinwheels

👥 12 | ⏱ 15 min | 🍽 15 min

Delicate puff pastry pinwheels filled with pesto and sourdough discard dough, perfect as an appetizer.

Ingredients:

- 1 cup sourdough discard
- 1 1/2 cups all-purpose flour
- 1/4 cup olive oil
- 1/2 cup prepared pesto

- 1/4 cup grated Parmesan cheese

Instructions:

1. Preheat the oven to 375°F (190°C) and line a baking sheet with parchment paper.
2. In a bowl, mix sourdough discard, flour, and olive oil to form a dough. Roll out the dough into a rectangle.
3. Spread the pesto evenly over the dough and sprinkle with Parmesan.
4. Roll up the dough tightly, slice into pinwheels, and place on the baking sheet.
5. Bake for 12-15 minutes until golden.

25. Sourdough Discard Onion Rings

👥 4 | ⏱ 15 min | 🍲 10 min

Crispy and tangy onion rings made with a sourdough discard batter.

Ingredients:

- 1 cup sourdough discard
- 1 cup all-purpose flour
- 1 large onion, sliced into rings
- 1/2 teaspoon salt
- 1/2 teaspoon garlic powder
- 1/2 cup cold water
- Oil for frying

Instructions:

1. Heat oil in a deep fryer or large pot to 350°F (175°C).
2. In a bowl, whisk together sourdough discard, flour, salt, garlic powder, and cold water to make a batter.
3. Dip each onion ring into the batter and fry in hot oil until golden brown, about 2-3 minutes per side.
4. Drain on paper towels and serve hot.

26. Sourdough Discard Zucchini Fritters

👥 4 | ⏱ 10 min | 🍲 10 min

Light and crispy zucchini fritters with a sourdough discard base, great as a snack or side dish.

Ingredients:

- 1 cup sourdough discard
- 2 medium zucchinis, grated
- 1/4 cup grated Parmesan cheese
- 1 egg
- 1/4 cup all-purpose flour
- 1 teaspoon salt
- 1/2 teaspoon black pepper
- Olive oil for frying

Instructions:

1. Squeeze out excess moisture from the grated zucchini.
2. In a bowl, mix sourdough discard, zucchini, Parmesan, egg, flour, salt, and pepper.
3. Heat olive oil in a skillet over medium heat. Drop spoonfuls of the batter into the skillet and flatten slightly.
4. Fry for 3-4 minutes per side until golden and crispy.

27. Sourdough Discard Stuffed Mushrooms

👥 12 | ⏱ 15 min | 🍲 20 min

Savory stuffed mushrooms with a sourdough discard and cheese filling.

Ingredients:

- 12 large button mushrooms, stems removed
- 1/2 cup sourdough discard
- 1/4 cup cream cheese, softened
- 1/4 cup grated Parmesan
- 1 clove garlic, minced

- 1 tablespoon chopped parsley
- Salt and pepper to taste

Instructions:

1. Preheat the oven to 375°F (190°C).
2. In a bowl, mix sourdough discard, cream cheese, Parmesan, garlic, parsley, salt, and pepper.
3. Stuff each mushroom with the sourdough filling and place on a baking sheet.
4. Bake for 20 minutes until the mushrooms are tender and the filling is golden.

28. Sourdough Discard Mini Quiches

👥 12 | ⏱ 15 min | 🍽 20 min

Mini quiches made with a sourdough discard crust, filled with cheese and vegetables.

Ingredients:

- 1 cup sourdough discard
- 1 1/2 cups all-purpose flour
- 1/4 cup cold butter, cubed
- 1/4 cup cold water
- 3 large eggs
- 1/2 cup shredded cheese
- 1/2 cup chopped vegetables (spinach, bell peppers, etc.)
- Salt and pepper to taste

Instructions:

1. Preheat the oven to 350°F (175°C) and grease a muffin tin.
2. In a bowl, mix sourdough discard, flour, butter, and cold water to form a dough. Roll out and cut into circles, pressing into the muffin cups.
3. In another bowl, whisk together eggs, cheese, vegetables, salt, and pepper. Pour the filling into each crust.
4. Bake for 20 minutes until set and golden.

29. Sourdough Discard Savory Pancakes

👥 4 | ⏱ 10 min | 🍽 10 min

Fluffy, savory pancakes made with sourdough discard, perfect for a snack or light meal.

Ingredients:

- 1 cup sourdough discard
- 1 cup all-purpose flour
- 1/2 teaspoon baking soda
- 1/4 teaspoon salt
- 1 large egg
- 1/2 cup milk
- 1/2 cup shredded cheese
- 1/4 cup chopped green onions
- Butter for cooking

Instructions:

1. In a bowl, mix sourdough discard, flour, baking soda, salt, egg, and milk until smooth.
2. Stir in the cheese and green onions.
3. Heat butter in a skillet over medium heat and drop spoonfuls of batter into the pan. Cook for 2-3 minutes per side until golden brown.

30. Sourdough Discard Garlic Breadsticks

👥 12 breadsticks | ⏱ 15 min | 🍽 12 min

Soft and garlicky breadsticks made with sourdough discard, perfect as a snack or appetizer.

Ingredients:

- 1 cup sourdough discard
- 2 1/2 cups all-purpose flour
- 1/4 cup olive oil
- 1 teaspoon salt
- 1 teaspoon instant yeast

- 1/2 cup warm water
- 1/4 cup melted butter
- 2 cloves garlic, minced

Instructions:

1. In a large bowl, mix sourdough discard, flour, olive oil, salt, yeast, and warm water. Knead until smooth and let rise for 1 hour.
2. Preheat the oven to 375°F (190°C).
3. Roll the dough into thin breadsticks and place on a baking sheet.
4. Bake for 10-12 minutes until golden.
5. Brush with melted butter mixed with garlic and garnish with parsley.

Chapter 6: Lunch & Dinner Favorites

1. Sourdough Discard Veggie Burgers

👥 4 | ⏱ 15 min | 🍲 20 min

These veggie burgers are hearty and flavorful, with a soft texture thanks to the sourdough discard. Serve on a bun with your favorite toppings.

Ingredients:

- 1 cup sourdough discard
- 1 1/2 cups cooked quinoa or rice
- 1/2 cup breadcrumbs
- 1/4 cup grated carrots
- 1/4 cup chopped spinach
- 1 egg
- 1 teaspoon cumin
- Salt and pepper to taste
- Olive oil for frying

Instructions:

1. In a large bowl, combine the sourdough discard, quinoa, breadcrumbs, carrots, spinach, egg, cumin, salt, and pepper. Mix until well combined.
2. Form the mixture into 4 patties.
3. Heat a tablespoon of olive oil in a skillet over medium heat. Fry the patties for 4-5 minutes on each side until golden and firm.
4. Serve on buns with your favorite toppings.

2. Sourdough Discard Chicken Pot Pie

👥 4 | ⏱ 20 min | 🍲 40 min

This comforting chicken pot pie is made with a flaky sourdough discard crust and a rich, creamy filling.

Ingredients:

- 1 cup sourdough discard
- 2 cups all-purpose flour
- 1/4 cup cold butter, cubed
- 1/4 teaspoon salt
- 1/4 cup cold water

For the Filling:

- 2 cups cooked chicken, shredded
- 1 cup frozen peas and carrots
- 1/2 cup chopped potatoes
- 1 cup chicken broth
- 1/2 cup milk
- 2 tablespoons butter
- 2 tablespoons all-purpose flour

Instructions:

1. Preheat the oven to 375°F (190°C).
2. In a bowl, mix the sourdough discard, flour, butter, salt, and cold water until a dough forms. Chill for 15 minutes.
3. In a skillet, melt the butter and whisk in the flour to make a roux. Slowly add the chicken broth and milk, stirring until thickened.
4. Add the chicken, peas, carrots, and potatoes. Cook for 5 minutes.
5. Roll out the dough and place it over the filling in a pie dish.
6. Bake for 35-40 minutes until the crust is golden brown.

3. Sourdough Discard Pizza Margherita

👥 4 | ⏱ 15 min (+ rise) | 🍲 15 min

This classic Margherita pizza has a crispy sourdough discard crust, topped with fresh mozzarella, basil, and tomatoes.

Ingredients:

- 1 cup sourdough discard
- 2 1/2 cups all-purpose flour
- 1 teaspoon yeast
- 1 teaspoon sugar
- 1/2 teaspoon salt
- 1/2 cup warm water

For the Topping:

- 1/2 cup pizza sauce
- 1 cup fresh mozzarella, sliced
- Fresh basil leaves
- Olive oil for drizzling

Instructions:

1. Mix the discard, flour, yeast, sugar, salt, and water into a dough. Knead for 10 minutes.
2. Let rise for 1 hour.
3. Preheat the oven to 450°F (230°C).
4. Roll out the dough, place it on a pizza stone, and spread the sauce. Top with mozzarella and basil.
5. Bake for 12-15 minutes until the crust is crispy and the cheese is melted. Drizzle with olive oil and serve.

4. Sourdough Discard Gnocchi

👥 4 | ⏱ 20 min | 🍲 10 min

These light and fluffy gnocchi are made with sourdough discard and potatoes, creating a delicate texture perfect for any sauce.

Ingredients:

- 1 cup sourdough discard
- 2 large potatoes, boiled and mashed
- 1 1/2 cups all-purpose flour
- 1 egg
- 1/2 teaspoon salt

Instructions:

1. In a large bowl, mix the sourdough discard, mashed potatoes, flour, egg, and salt until a soft dough forms.
2. Roll the dough into long ropes and cut into small pieces.
3. Bring a large pot of salted water to a boil. Cook the gnocchi in batches until they float to the surface, about 2-3 minutes.
4. Drain and toss with your favorite sauce, such as marinara or pesto.

5. Sourdough Discard Veggie Tacos

👥 4 | ⏱ 10 min | 🍲 10 min

These veggie tacos are filled with roasted vegetables and served in soft sourdough discard tortillas.

Ingredients:

- 1 cup sourdough discard
- 2 cups all-purpose flour
- 1/2 teaspoon baking powder
- 1/2 teaspoon salt
- 1/4 cup warm water
- 1 zucchini, sliced
- 1 bell pepper, sliced
- 1/2 onion, sliced
- Olive oil for roasting
- Taco toppings: sour cream, salsa, cheese

Instructions:

1. In a bowl, mix the discard, flour, baking powder, salt, and water until a dough forms.
2. Divide the dough into small balls and roll each into a tortilla.
3. Heat a skillet and cook each tortilla for 1-2 minutes per side.
4. Toss the veggies with olive oil, roast at 400°F (200°C) for 15 minutes, and serve with tortillas and taco toppings.

6. Sourdough Discard Spinach Lasagna

👥 6 | ⏱ 20 min | 🍲 45 min

This creamy spinach lasagna is layered with sourdough discard pasta sheets, ricotta, and mozzarella.

Ingredients:

- 1 cup sourdough discard
- 2 cups all-purpose flour
- 1/2 teaspoon salt
- 3 large eggs

For the Filling:

- 2 cups ricotta cheese
- 2 cups fresh spinach, cooked and drained
- 1 cup shredded mozzarella
- 2 cups marinara sauce

Instructions:

1. In a bowl, mix the discard, flour, salt, and eggs to form a pasta dough. Roll out thin and cut into lasagna sheets.
2. Preheat the oven to 375°F (190°C).
3. In a baking dish, layer the lasagna sheets, ricotta, spinach, mozzarella, and marinara sauce.
4. Repeat the layers and finish with a layer of cheese.
5. Bake for 40-45 minutes until bubbling and golden.

7. Sourdough Discard Veggie Frittata

👥 4 | ⏱ 10 min | 🍲 20 min

This light, fluffy frittata is packed with vegetables and made even better with a sourdough discard base.

Ingredients:

- 1 cup sourdough discard
- 4 large eggs
- 1/2 cup milk
- 1/2 cup chopped spinach
- 1/2 cup diced bell pepper
- 1/4 cup chopped onion
- 1/2 cup shredded cheese
- Salt and pepper to taste

Instructions:

1. Preheat the oven to 350°F (175°C).
2. In a large bowl, whisk together the sourdough discard, eggs, milk, salt, and pepper.
3. Stir in the spinach, bell pepper, onion, and cheese.
4. Pour the mixture into a greased oven-safe skillet and bake for 20-25 minutes until set.

8. Sourdough Discard Stuffed Bell Peppers

👥 4 | ⏱ 15 min | 🍲 30 min

These bell peppers are stuffed with a flavorful mixture of rice, beans, and sourdough discard, then baked to perfection.

Ingredients:

- 4 large bell peppers
- 1 cup cooked rice
- 1/2 cup sourdough discard
- 1/2 cup black beans
- 1/2 cup corn
- 1/2 cup shredded cheese
- 1/2 teaspoon cumin
- Salt and pepper to taste

Instructions:

1. Preheat the oven to 375°F (190°C).
2. Slice the tops off the bell peppers and remove the seeds.
3. In a bowl, mix the rice, sourdough discard, beans, corn, cheese, cumin, salt, and pepper.

4. Stuff the peppers with the mixture and place them in a baking dish.
5. Bake for 25-30 minutes until the peppers are tender.

9. Sourdough Discard Shepherd's Pie

👥 6 | ⏱ 20 min | 🍲 40 min

This hearty shepherd's pie features a savory beef and vegetable filling, topped with mashed potatoes mixed with sourdough discard.

Ingredients:

- 1 lb ground beef
- 1 cup frozen peas and carrots
- 1 onion, chopped
- 1 tablespoon Worcestershire sauce
- 1 cup beef broth
- 1 cup mashed potatoes
- 1/2 cup sourdough discard
- 1/2 cup shredded cheese

Instructions:

1. Preheat the oven to 375°F (190°C).
2. In a skillet, brown the ground beef with the onions. Add the peas, carrots, Worcestershire sauce, and broth, and simmer for 5 minutes.
3. Mix the mashed potatoes with the sourdough discard.
4. Transfer the beef mixture to a baking dish, top with the mashed potatoes, and sprinkle with cheese.
5. Bake for 30-40 minutes until golden.

10. Sourdough Discard Flatbread Pizza

👥 4 | ⏱ 15 min | 🍲 10 min

This quick flatbread pizza is perfect for a fast lunch or dinner, with a tangy sourdough discard base and your favorite toppings.

Ingredients:

- 1 cup sourdough discard
- 1 1/2 cups all-purpose flour
- 1/4 teaspoon salt
- 1/4 cup water
- 1 tablespoon olive oil
- Pizza toppings of your choice

Instructions:

1. Preheat the oven to 450°F (230°C).
2. Mix the sourdough discard, flour, salt, water, and olive oil until a dough forms.
3. Roll out the dough into a flat round and place on a baking sheet.
4. Top with your favorite pizza toppings and bake for 10-12 minutes until crispy.

11. Sourdough Discard Meatloaf

👥 6 | ⏱ 15 min | 🍲 1 hr

This classic meatloaf recipe uses sourdough discard as a binder, adding moisture and a slight tang.

Ingredients:

- 1 lb ground beef
- 1/2 cup sourdough discard
- 1/2 cup breadcrumbs
- 1 egg
- 1/4 cup ketchup
- 1/4 cup chopped onion
- 1 teaspoon Worcestershire sauce
- Salt and pepper to taste

Instructions:

1. Preheat the oven to 350°F (175°C).
2. In a large bowl, mix the ground beef, sourdough discard, breadcrumbs, egg, ketchup, onion, Worcestershire sauce, salt, and pepper.
3. Shape the mixture into a loaf and place in a greased baking dish.
4. Bake for 1 hour, basting with additional ketchup halfway through.

12. Sourdough Discard Chicken Enchiladas

👥 4 | ⏱ 20 min | 🍲 30 min

These cheesy chicken enchiladas are wrapped in sourdough discard tortillas and smothered in a spicy sauce.

Ingredients:

- 1 cup sourdough discard
- 2 cups all-purpose flour
- 1/2 teaspoon baking powder
- 1/4 cup warm water
- 2 cups cooked shredded chicken
- 1 cup shredded cheese
- 2 cups enchilada sauce

Instructions:

1. In a bowl, mix the discard, flour, baking powder, and water until a dough forms.
2. Roll out the dough into tortillas and cook in a hot skillet for 1-2 minutes per side.
3. Preheat the oven to 375°F (190°C).
4. Fill each tortilla with chicken and cheese, roll up, and place in a baking dish. Pour the enchilada sauce over the top.
5. Bake for 25-30 minutes until bubbly.

13. Sourdough Discard Quiche

👥 6 | ⏱ 20 min | 🍲 45 min

This rich, savory quiche has a sourdough discard crust and a creamy filling of eggs, cheese, and vegetables.

Ingredients:

- 1 cup sourdough discard
- 2 cups all-purpose flour
- 1/2 cup cold butter, cubed
- 1/4 cup cold water

For the Filling:

- 4 large eggs

- 1 cup milk
- 1/2 cup shredded cheese
- 1 cup cooked spinach
- Salt and pepper to taste

Instructions:

1. Preheat the oven to 375°F (190°C).
2. In a bowl, mix the discard, flour, butter, and water to form a dough. Chill for 15 minutes.
3. Roll out the dough and place in a pie dish.
4. In a separate bowl, whisk the eggs, milk, cheese, spinach, salt, and pepper. Pour into the crust.
5. Bake for 40-45 minutes until set.

14. Sourdough Discard Vegetable Stir-Fry

👥 4 | ⏱ 10 min | 🍲 10 min

This quick stir-fry is loaded with fresh vegetables and tossed in a savory sauce, served with sourdough discard flatbreads.

Ingredients:

- 1 cup sourdough discard
- 2 cups all-purpose flour
- 1/4 teaspoon salt
- 1/4 cup water
- 1 tablespoon olive oil

For the Stir-Fry:

- 1 bell pepper, sliced
- 1 carrot, sliced
- 1 zucchini, sliced
- 1/4 cup soy sauce
- 1 tablespoon honey
- 1 teaspoon ginger
- 1 clove garlic, minced

Instructions:

1. Mix the discard, flour, salt, water, and olive oil into a dough. Roll into flatbreads

and cook in a skillet for 2-3 minutes per side.

2. In a hot wok or skillet, stir-fry the vegetables with garlic and ginger.
3. Add the soy sauce and honey, and toss to coat.
4. Serve the stir-fry with the sourdough flatbreads.

15. Sourdough Discard BBQ Chicken Pizza

👥 4 | ⏱ 10 min (+ rise) | 🍽 12 min

This BBQ chicken pizza features a tangy sourdough discard crust, topped with BBQ sauce, chicken, and cheese.

Ingredients:

- 1 cup sourdough discard
- 2 1/2 cups all-purpose flour
- 1 teaspoon yeast
- 1 teaspoon sugar
- 1/2 teaspoon salt
- 1/2 cup warm water

For the Topping:

- 1/2 cup BBQ sauce
- 1 cup cooked shredded chicken
- 1 cup shredded mozzarella
- Red onion, sliced
- Fresh cilantro for garnish

Instructions:

1. Mix the discard, flour, yeast, sugar, salt, and water into a dough. Knead for 10 minutes and let rise for 1 hour.
2. Preheat the oven to 450°F (230°C).
3. Roll out the dough, top with BBQ sauce, chicken, cheese, and onions.
4. Bake for 12-15 minutes until the crust is crispy. Garnish with cilantro.

16. Sourdough Discard Chicken and Dumplings

👥 6 | ⏱ 20 min | 🍽 30 min

This comforting chicken and dumplings dish is made with sourdough discard dumplings, creating a fluffy texture.

Ingredients:

- 1 cup sourdough discard
- 2 cups all-purpose flour
- 1 tablespoon baking powder
- 1/2 teaspoon salt
- 1/2 cup milk
- 1 lb cooked shredded chicken
- 1 cup chicken broth
- 1/2 cup carrots, sliced
- 1/2 cup celery, sliced
- 1 onion, chopped

Instructions:

1. In a large pot, sauté the onions, carrots, and celery until softened.
2. Add the chicken and broth, and bring to a simmer.
3. In a bowl, mix the discard, flour, baking powder, salt, and milk until a dough forms.
4. Drop spoonfuls of the dough into the simmering soup, cover, and cook for 15 minutes until the dumplings are cooked through.

17. Sourdough Discard Fish Tacos

👥 4 | ⏱ 15 min | 🍽 10 min

These crispy fish tacos are served with sourdough discard tortillas and topped with a tangy slaw.

Ingredients:

- 1 cup sourdough discard
- 2 cups all-purpose flour

- 1/2 teaspoon baking powder
- 1/4 cup warm water
- 4 fish fillets (cod or tilapia)
- 1/2 cup flour (for dredging)
- Oil for frying

For the Slaw:

- 1 cup shredded cabbage
- 1 tablespoon mayonnaise
- 1 tablespoon lime juice
- Salt and pepper to taste

Instructions:

1. Mix the discard, flour, baking powder, and water into a dough. Roll out into tortillas and cook in a skillet for 1-2 minutes per side.
2. Dredge the fish fillets in flour and fry in hot oil until golden, about 3-4 minutes per side.
3. In a bowl, mix the slaw ingredients.
4. Serve the fish in the tortillas with slaw and your favorite toppings.

18. Sourdough Discard Beef Stroganoff

👥 4 | ⏱ 15 min | 🍲 25 min

This creamy beef stroganoff is made with sourdough discard noodles, creating a comforting and hearty dish.

Ingredients:

- 1 cup sourdough discard
- 2 cups all-purpose flour
- 1/2 teaspoon salt
- 1/4 cup water

For the Stroganoff:

- 1 lb beef strips
- 1/2 cup sour cream
- 1/2 cup beef broth
- 1/2 onion, chopped

- 1 tablespoon butter
- 1/2 cup mushrooms, sliced

Instructions:

1. Mix the discard, flour, salt, and water to form a pasta dough. Roll out and cut into noodles.
2. In a skillet, cook the beef and onions in butter until browned. Add the mushrooms and cook for 5 minutes.
3. Stir in the broth and sour cream, and simmer for 10 minutes.
4. Cook the noodles in boiling water for 3-4 minutes, then toss with the beef mixture.

19. Sourdough Discard Pork Buns

👥 8 buns | ⏱ 15 min (+ rise) | 🍲 25 min

These fluffy pork buns are filled with savory pork and vegetables, with a soft sourdough discard dough.

Ingredients:

- 1 cup sourdough discard
- 2 1/2 cups all-purpose flour
- 1 teaspoon yeast
- 1/2 teaspoon sugar
- 1/2 teaspoon salt
- 1/4 cup warm water

For the Filling:

- 1 cup cooked pork, shredded
- 1/2 cup chopped cabbage
- 1 tablespoon soy sauce
- 1 tablespoon hoisin sauce

Instructions:

1. Mix the discard, flour, yeast, sugar, salt, and water into a dough. Knead for 10 minutes and let rise for 1 hour.
2. Preheat the oven to 375°F (190°C).

3. Roll out the dough into circles and fill with the pork and cabbage mixture.
4. Fold and seal the buns, then bake for 20-25 minutes until golden.

20. Sourdough Discard Beef Wellington

👥 4 | ⏱ 30 min | 🍲 40 min

This elegant dish features tender beef wrapped in a sourdough discard pastry crust, perfect for special occasions.

Ingredients:

- 1 cup sourdough discard
- 2 cups all-purpose flour
- 1/2 cup cold butter, cubed
- 1/4 cup cold water
- 4 beef tenderloin steaks
- 1/2 cup mushrooms, finely chopped
- 1 tablespoon Dijon mustard
- 1 egg (for egg wash)

Instructions:

1. In a bowl, mix the discard, flour, butter, and water until a dough forms. Chill for 30 minutes.
2. Preheat the oven to 400°F (200°C).
3. Sear the beef steaks on all sides and spread each with Dijon mustard.
4. Roll out the dough, place the steak in the center, and top with mushrooms. Fold the dough around the steak.
5. Brush with egg wash and bake for 20-25 minutes until golden and crispy.

21. Sourdough Discard Veggie Quesadillas

👥 4 | ⏱ 10 min | 🍲 10 min

A quick and delicious lunch with crispy sourdough discard tortillas and a filling of mixed veggies and cheese.

Ingredients:

- 1 cup sourdough discard
- 2 cups all-purpose flour
- 1/2 teaspoon salt
- 1/4 cup water
- 1 cup shredded cheese
- 1/2 cup sautéed bell peppers and onions
- 1/2 cup cooked black beans
- Salsa for serving

Instructions:

1. Mix sourdough discard, flour, salt, and water to form a dough. Divide and roll into tortillas.
2. Cook the tortillas on a hot skillet until golden, about 1-2 minutes per side.
3. Fill each tortilla with sautéed veggies, black beans, and cheese. Fold and cook until the cheese is melted.
4. Serve with salsa on the side.

22. Sourdough Discard Grilled Cheese Sandwich

👥 2 | ⏱ 5 min | 🍲 10 min

Classic grilled cheese with a tangy sourdough discard twist.

Ingredients:

- 4 slices sourdough discard bread (or regular bread with sourdough discard added to the dough)
- 4 slices cheddar cheese
- 2 tablespoons butter
- 1/4 teaspoon garlic powder (optional)

Instructions:

1. Butter one side of each bread slice. Sprinkle garlic powder on the buttered side for extra flavor.
2. Place two slices of cheese between two slices of bread, buttered side out.

3. Heat a skillet over medium heat and grill the sandwich until golden on both sides and the cheese is melted, about 3-4 minutes per side.

23. Sourdough Discard Veggie Burger

👥 4 | ⏱ 15 min | 🍽 20 min

A healthy, hearty veggie burger with sourdough discard adding a tangy flavor to the patty mixture.

Ingredients:

- 1 cup sourdough discard
- 1 can black beans, drained and mashed
- 1/2 cup breadcrumbs
- 1/2 cup shredded carrot
- 1/4 cup finely chopped onion
- 1 tablespoon soy sauce
- 1 teaspoon cumin
- Salt and pepper to taste
- Olive oil for cooking

Instructions:

1. In a bowl, combine sourdough discard, mashed black beans, breadcrumbs, shredded carrot, onion, soy sauce, cumin, salt, and pepper. Form into 4 patties.
2. Heat olive oil in a skillet and cook the patties for 4-5 minutes per side, until browned and cooked through.
3. Serve on buns with your favorite toppings.

24. Sourdough Discard Veggie Wraps

👥 4 | ⏱ 10 min | 🍽 5 min

A light, refreshing wrap using sourdough discard flatbreads, packed with fresh veggies and hummus.

Ingredients:

- 1 cup sourdough discard
- 2 cups all-purpose flour
- 1/4 teaspoon salt
- 1/2 cup water
- 1/2 cup hummus
- 1 cucumber, sliced
- 1 bell pepper, sliced
- 1/2 cup shredded carrots
- 1 cup fresh spinach

Instructions:

1. Mix sourdough discard, flour, salt, and water to form a dough. Divide and roll into thin wraps.
2. Cook the wraps on a skillet for 1-2 minutes on each side.
3. Spread each wrap with hummus and layer with cucumber, bell pepper, carrots, and spinach. Roll up and serve.

25. Sourdough Discard Tomato Soup

👥 4 | ⏱ 10 min | 🍽 25 min

A comforting bowl of tomato soup with the added flavor of sourdough discard.

Ingredients:

- 1 cup sourdough discard
- 2 cans (14 oz each) crushed tomatoes
- 1/2 onion, chopped
- 2 cloves garlic, minced
- 1 cup vegetable broth
- 1 tablespoon olive oil
- 1 teaspoon dried basil
- Salt and pepper to taste

Instructions:

1. Heat olive oil in a pot and sauté the onion and garlic until soft, about 5 minutes.

2. Add the crushed tomatoes, vegetable broth, sourdough discard, basil, salt, and pepper. Simmer for 20 minutes.
3. Use an immersion blender to puree the soup until smooth. Serve hot.

26. Frittata

👥 4 | ⏱ 10 min | 🍲 20 min

A versatile, quick frittata made with sourdough discard and seasonal vegetables.

Ingredients:

- 1 cup sourdough discard
- 6 large eggs
- 1 cup mixed vegetables (zucchini, bell peppers, spinach)
- 1/2 cup shredded cheese
- 1 tablespoon olive oil
- Salt and pepper to taste

Instructions:

1. Preheat the oven to 375°F (190°C).
2. In a skillet, sauté vegetables in olive oil until tender.
3. Whisk together eggs, sourdough discard, salt, and pepper. Pour the mixture over the vegetables.
4. Sprinkle with cheese and bake for 15-20 minutes until set.

27. Sourdough Discard Chicken Salad

👥 4 | ⏱ 10 min | 🍲 N/A

A light, refreshing chicken salad with a tangy sourdough discard dressing.

Ingredients:

- 2 cups cooked chicken, shredded
- 1/4 cup sourdough discard
- 1/4 cup mayonnaise
- 1 tablespoon Dijon mustard
- 1 tablespoon lemon juice
- 1/4 cup chopped celery
- Salt and pepper to taste

Instructions:

1. In a bowl, mix sourdough discard, mayonnaise, mustard, lemon juice, salt, and pepper to make the dressing.
2. Toss the shredded chicken and celery in the dressing.
3. Serve on a bed of lettuce or in sandwiches.

28. Sourdough Discard Falafel

👥 4 | ⏱ 15 min | 🍲 15 min

Crispy, flavorful falafel patties with a sourdough discard base, perfect for lunch wraps or salads.

Ingredients:

- 1 cup sourdough discard
- 1 can (15 oz) chickpeas, drained and mashed
- 1/4 cup chopped parsley
- 1/4 cup breadcrumbs
- 2 cloves garlic, minced
- 1 teaspoon cumin
- Salt and pepper to taste
- Olive oil for cooking

Instructions:

1. In a bowl, combine sourdough discard, mashed chickpeas, parsley, breadcrumbs, garlic, cumin, salt, and pepper. Form into small patties.
2. Heat olive oil in a skillet and cook the falafel patties for 3-4 minutes per side until golden and crispy.
3. Serve in pita bread or on a salad with tahini sauce.

29. Sourdough Discard Spinach Quiche

👥 6 | ⏱ 15 min | 🍽 30 min

A delicious spinach quiche made with a sourdough discard crust.

Ingredients:

- 1 cup sourdough discard
- 1 1/2 cups all-purpose flour
- 1/2 teaspoon salt
- 1/4 cup cold butter, cubed
- 2 tablespoons cold water
- 1 cup fresh spinach, chopped
- 1/2 cup shredded cheese
- 4 large eggs
- 1/2 cup milk
- Salt and pepper to taste

Instructions:

1. Preheat the oven to 350°F (175°C).
2. In a bowl, combine sourdough discard, flour, salt, and butter until crumbly. Add water and form a dough. Press into a pie dish.
3. In another bowl, whisk together eggs, milk, spinach, cheese, salt, and pepper. Pour into the crust.
4. Bake for 30 minutes or until set.

30. Sourdough Discard Veggie Stir-Fry

👥 4 | ⏱ 10 min | 🍽 15 min

A quick and easy stir-fry with a sourdough discard-based sauce for a tangy twist.

Ingredients:

- 1 cup sourdough discard
- 1/4 cup soy sauce
- 1 tablespoon honey
- 1 tablespoon rice vinegar
- 1 tablespoon sesame oil
- 1 bell pepper, sliced
- 1 carrot, sliced
- 1/2 cup broccoli florets
- 2 tablespoons olive oil
- Cooked rice for serving

Instructions:

1. In a bowl, whisk together sourdough discard, soy sauce, honey, rice vinegar, and sesame oil to make the sauce.
2. Heat olive oil in a skillet and sauté the bell pepper, carrot, and broccoli for 5-7 minutes.
3. Add the sauce and cook for another 5 minutes, stirring frequently.
4. Serve over cooked rice.

31. Sourdough Discard Lasagna

👥 6 | ⏱ 20 min | 🍽 1 hr

A classic Italian dish with layers of sourdough discard noodles, rich tomato sauce, and cheese.

Ingredients:

- 1 cup sourdough discard
- 1 1/2 cups all-purpose flour
- 1/2 teaspoon salt
- 2 eggs
- 2 cups marinara sauce
- 1 lb ground beef or turkey
- 2 cups ricotta cheese
- 2 cups shredded mozzarella
- 1/4 cup grated Parmesan

Instructions:

1. Preheat the oven to 375°F (190°C).
2. In a bowl, mix sourdough discard, flour, salt, and eggs to form a pasta dough. Roll it out and cut into lasagna noodles.
3. Brown the ground meat in a skillet, then stir in marinara sauce.

4. In a baking dish, layer lasagna noodles, meat sauce, ricotta, and mozzarella. Repeat layers and top with Parmesan.
5. Cover with foil and bake for 45 minutes. Remove foil and bake for an additional 15 minutes until golden and bubbly.

32. Sourdough Discard Pizza Margherita

👥 4 | ⏱ 15 min | 🍲 20 min

A classic pizza with a crispy sourdough discard crust, topped with fresh mozzarella, basil, and tomatoes.

Ingredients:

- 1 cup sourdough discard
- 1 1/2 cups all-purpose flour
- 1/2 teaspoon salt
- 1/2 cup warm water
- 1 tablespoon olive oil
- 1/2 cup tomato sauce
- 1 cup fresh mozzarella, sliced
- Fresh basil leaves
- 2 tomatoes, sliced
- Salt and pepper to taste

Instructions:

1. Preheat the oven to 475°F (245°C).
2. In a bowl, mix sourdough discard, flour, salt, water, and olive oil to form a dough. Roll it out and place on a pizza stone or baking sheet.
3. Spread tomato sauce over the dough, and layer with sliced tomatoes and mozzarella.
4. Bake for 15-20 minutes until the crust is crispy and the cheese is melted. Top with fresh basil before serving.

33. Sourdough Discard Stuffed Bell Peppers

👥 4 | ⏱ 20 min | 🍲 30 min

Bell peppers stuffed with a flavorful mix of sourdough discard, rice, and ground meat, topped with melted cheese.

Ingredients:

- 4 bell peppers, tops cut off and seeds removed
- 1/2 cup sourdough discard
- 1/2 cup cooked rice
- 1/2 lb ground beef or turkey
- 1 small onion, chopped
- 1/2 cup tomato sauce
- 1 teaspoon Italian seasoning
- 1 cup shredded cheese
- Salt and pepper to taste

Instructions:

1. Preheat the oven to 375°F (190°C).
2. In a skillet, cook ground meat and onion until browned. Stir in the rice, sourdough discard, tomato sauce, Italian seasoning, salt, and pepper.
3. Stuff the mixture into the bell peppers and place them in a baking dish.
4. Cover with foil and bake for 20 minutes. Remove the foil, top with shredded cheese, and bake for another 10 minutes.

34. Sourdough Discard Chicken Pot Pie

👥 6 | ⏱ 20 min | 🍲 40 min

A comforting dish of tender chicken and vegetables in a creamy sauce, topped with a flaky sourdough discard crust.

Ingredients:

- 1 cup sourdough discard
- 1 1/2 cups all-purpose flour

- 1/2 cup cold butter, cubed
- 1/4 cup cold water
- 2 cups cooked chicken, shredded
- 1/2 cup peas and carrots (frozen or fresh)
- 1/2 cup diced potatoes
- 1 cup chicken broth
- 1/2 cup milk
- 1 tablespoon flour (for thickening)
- Salt and pepper to taste

Instructions:

1. Preheat the oven to 400°F (200°C).
2. In a pot, combine chicken, peas, carrots, potatoes, chicken broth, and milk. Simmer until the potatoes are soft. Stir in flour to thicken the sauce, and season with salt and pepper.
3. In a bowl, mix sourdough discard, flour, butter, and water to form a dough. Roll out the dough and place it over the chicken mixture in a baking dish.
4. Bake for 30-40 minutes until the crust is golden and crisp.

35. Sourdough Discard Shrimp Scampi

👥 4 | ⏱ 10 min | 🍲 15 min

A quick and easy shrimp scampi made with a sourdough discard-based garlic butter sauce.

Ingredients:

- 1/2 cup sourdough discard
- 1 lb shrimp, peeled and deveined
- 1/4 cup butter
- 4 cloves garlic, minced
- 1/4 cup white wine or chicken broth
- 1 tablespoon lemon juice
- 2 tablespoons chopped parsley
- Salt and pepper to taste
- Cooked pasta for serving

Instructions:

1. In a large skillet, melt butter and sauté garlic for 1 minute.
2. Add shrimp and cook for 2-3 minutes until pink.
3. Stir in the sourdough discard, white wine, lemon juice, parsley, salt, and pepper. Simmer for 5 minutes.
4. Serve over cooked pasta.

36. Sourdough Discard Beef Stew

👥 6 | ⏱ 15 min | 🍲 2 hr

A hearty beef stew with sourdough discard adding depth to the broth.

Ingredients:

- 1 cup sourdough discard
- 1 lb beef stew meat, cubed
- 2 carrots, sliced
- 2 potatoes, cubed
- 1 onion, chopped
- 2 cloves garlic, minced
- 4 cups beef broth
- 1 tablespoon tomato paste
- 1 teaspoon thyme
- Salt and pepper to taste

Instructions:

1. In a large pot, brown the beef stew meat on all sides.
2. Add the onion, garlic, carrots, and potatoes, and sauté for 5 minutes.
3. Stir in beef broth, tomato paste, thyme, salt, pepper, and sourdough discard.
4. Cover and simmer for 1.5-2 hours until the meat is tender and the vegetables are cooked through.

37. Sourdough Discard Eggplant Parmesan

👥 4 | ⏱ 20 min | 🍲 40 min

Crispy layers of eggplant with sourdough discard breading, baked with marinara and cheese.

Ingredients:

- 2 large eggplants, sliced
- 1 cup sourdough discard
- 1 cup breadcrumbs
- 1/2 cup grated Parmesan cheese
- 2 cups marinara sauce
- 2 cups shredded mozzarella
- Olive oil for frying
- Salt and pepper to taste

Instructions:

1. Preheat the oven to 375°F (190°C).
2. Dip the eggplant slices in sourdough discard, then coat with breadcrumbs and Parmesan.
3. Fry the eggplant slices in olive oil until golden, then layer them in a baking dish with marinara sauce and mozzarella.
4. Bake for 30-40 minutes until bubbly and golden.

38. Sourdough Discard Turkey Meatballs

👥 4 | ⏱ 15 min | 🍲 30 min

Tender turkey meatballs with sourdough discard, served over spaghetti or on their own.

Ingredients:

- 1 cup sourdough discard
- 1 lb ground turkey
- 1/2 cup breadcrumbs
- 1/4 cup grated Parmesan
- 1 egg
- 2 cloves garlic, minced
- 1 tablespoon parsley
- Salt and pepper to taste
- Marinara sauce for serving

Instructions:

1. Preheat the oven to 375°F (190°C).
2. In a bowl, combine sourdough discard, ground turkey, breadcrumbs, Parmesan, egg, garlic, parsley, salt, and pepper.
3. Form the mixture into meatballs and place them on a baking sheet.
4. Bake for 25-30 minutes until cooked through. Serve with marinara sauce over pasta or as a main dish.

39. Sourdough Discard Chicken Tenders

👥 4 | ⏱ 10 min | 🍲 15 min

Crispy baked chicken tenders with a sourdough discard coating, perfect for a family dinner.

Ingredients:

- 1 cup sourdough discard
- 1 lb chicken tenders
- 1 cup breadcrumbs
- 1/2 cup grated Parmesan
- 1 teaspoon paprika
- Salt and pepper to taste
- Olive oil for drizzling

Instructions:

1. Preheat the oven to 400°F (200°C).
2. Dip each chicken tender in sourdough discard, then coat with breadcrumbs, Parmesan, paprika, salt, and pepper.
3. Place on a baking sheet, drizzle with olive oil, and bake for 12-15 minutes until golden and cooked through.

40. Sourdough Discard Beef Tacos

👥 4 | ⏱ 10 min | 🍽 15 min

Taco night made easy with sourdough discard tortillas and a flavorful beef filling.

Ingredients:

- 1 cup sourdough discard
- 2 cups all-purpose flour
- 1/2 teaspoon salt
- 1/4 cup water
- 1 lb ground beef
- 1 tablespoon taco seasoning
- 1/4 cup tomato sauce
- Shredded lettuce, cheese, and salsa for toppings

Instructions:

1. In a bowl, mix sourdough discard, flour, salt, and water to form a dough. Roll into small tortillas and cook in a hot skillet until golden.
2. Brown the ground beef in a skillet and stir in taco seasoning and tomato sauce. Cook for 5 minutes.
3. Fill the tortillas with beef and top with lettuce, cheese, and salsa.

Chapter 7: Sourdough Sweets

1. Sourdough Discard Chocolate Chip Cookies

👥 24 cookies | ⏱ 15 min | 🍲 12 min

These classic chocolate chip cookies get an upgrade with sourdough discard, adding a subtle tang that pairs perfectly with the sweetness.

Ingredients:

- 1/2 cup sourdough discard
- 1 1/2 cups all-purpose flour
- 1/2 cup butter, softened
- 1/2 cup brown sugar
- 1/4 cup white sugar
- 1 large egg
- 1 teaspoon vanilla extract
- 1/2 teaspoon baking soda
- 1/4 teaspoon salt
- 1 cup chocolate chips

Instructions:

1. Preheat the oven to 350°F (175°C) and line a baking sheet with parchment paper.
2. In a large bowl, cream together the butter, brown sugar, and white sugar until light and fluffy.
3. Mix in the sourdough discard, egg, and vanilla extract.
4. In a separate bowl, whisk together the flour, baking soda, and salt. Gradually add to the wet ingredients.
5. Stir in the chocolate chips.
6. Drop spoonfuls of dough onto the prepared baking sheet and bake for 10-12 minutes until golden.

2. Sourdough Discard Brownies

👥 16 brownies | ⏱ 10 min | 🍲 25 min

These fudgy brownies are rich and decadent, with a hint of sourdough tang that elevates the chocolate flavor.

Ingredients:

- 1/2 cup sourdough discard
- 1/2 cup butter, melted
- 1 cup sugar
- 2 large eggs
- 1 teaspoon vanilla extract
- 1/2 cup cocoa powder
- 1/2 cup all-purpose flour
- 1/2 teaspoon baking powder
- 1/4 teaspoon salt

Instructions:

1. Preheat the oven to 350°F (175°C) and grease an 8x8-inch baking pan.
2. In a large bowl, mix the melted butter and sugar until combined. Add the eggs and vanilla, stirring until smooth.
3. Stir in the sourdough discard.
4. In another bowl, whisk together the cocoa powder, flour, baking powder, and salt. Add to the wet ingredients and stir until just combined.
5. Pour the batter into the prepared pan and bake for 20-25 minutes.

3. Sourdough Discard Cinnamon Rolls

👥 12 rolls | ⏱ 30 min (+ rise) | 🍲 25 min

These soft, gooey cinnamon rolls are made with a sourdough discard dough, giving them a deeper flavor than traditional versions.

Ingredients:

- 1 cup sourdough discard
- 3 cups all-purpose flour
- 1/2 cup warm milk
- 1/4 cup sugar
- 1/4 cup melted butter
- 1 large egg
- 2 teaspoons instant yeast
- 1/2 teaspoon salt

For the Filling:

- 1/4 cup melted butter
- 1/2 cup brown sugar
- 2 tablespoons cinnamon

Instructions:

1. In a large bowl, combine the sourdough discard, flour, milk, sugar, melted butter, egg, yeast, and salt. Stir until a soft dough forms.
2. Knead for about 8 minutes until smooth and elastic. Let rise for 1-2 hours until doubled in size.
3. Roll out the dough into a rectangle, spread with melted butter, and sprinkle with brown sugar and cinnamon.
4. Roll the dough tightly, cut into 12 rolls, and place in a greased baking dish. Let rise for another 30 minutes.
5. Preheat the oven to 350°F (175°C) and bake for 20-25 minutes until golden.

4. Sourdough Discard Banana Bread

👥 8 | ⏱ 10 min | 🍽 50 min

This moist banana bread is enhanced with sourdough discard, adding a slight tang that balances the sweetness of the bananas.

Ingredients:

- 1 cup sourdough discard
- 2 ripe bananas, mashed

- 1/2 cup sugar
- 1/2 cup vegetable oil
- 2 large eggs
- 1 teaspoon vanilla extract
- 1 1/2 cups all-purpose flour
- 1 teaspoon baking soda
- 1/2 teaspoon salt
- 1/2 teaspoon cinnamon

Instructions:

1. Preheat the oven to 350°F (175°C) and grease a loaf pan.
2. In a large bowl, whisk together the sourdough discard, bananas, sugar, oil, eggs, and vanilla.
3. In another bowl, combine the flour, baking soda, salt, and cinnamon. Add to the wet ingredients and stir until just combined.
4. Pour the batter into the prepared loaf pan and bake for 50-55 minutes.

5. Sourdough Discard Chocolate Cake

👥 8 | ⏱ 15 min | 🍽 35 min

This rich chocolate cake has a tender crumb and a subtle sourdough flavor that enhances the chocolate.

Ingredients:

- 1 cup sourdough discard
- 1 cup all-purpose flour
- 1 cup sugar
- 1/2 cup cocoa powder
- 1 teaspoon baking soda
- 1/2 teaspoon salt
- 1 cup milk
- 1/2 cup vegetable oil
- 1 teaspoon vanilla extract
- 1 large egg

Instructions:

1. Preheat the oven to 350°F (175°C) and grease a 9-inch round cake pan.

2. In a large bowl, whisk together the flour, sugar, cocoa powder, baking soda, and salt.
3. Add the milk, oil, vanilla, egg, and sourdough discard. Stir until smooth.
4. Pour the batter into the prepared pan and bake for 30-35 minutes.

6. Sourdough Discard Lemon Bars

👥 16 bars | ⏱ 20 min | 🍲 25 min

These tangy lemon bars have a buttery sourdough discard crust, topped with a sweet and tart lemon filling.

Ingredients:

- 1 cup sourdough discard
- 1 1/2 cups all-purpose flour
- 1/2 cup powdered sugar
- 1/2 cup butter, cold and cubed
- 1/4 teaspoon salt

For the Lemon Filling:

- 4 large eggs
- 1 1/2 cups sugar
- 1/2 cup lemon juice
- 1/4 cup all-purpose flour

Instructions:

1. Preheat the oven to 350°F (175°C) and grease a 9x9-inch baking dish.
2. In a bowl, mix the sourdough discard, flour, powdered sugar, butter, and salt until a crumbly dough forms. Press into the baking dish and bake for 15 minutes.
3. In a separate bowl, whisk together the eggs, sugar, lemon juice, and flour. Pour over the crust and bake for another 20-25 minutes.

7. Sourdough Discard Apple Crumble

👥 6 | ⏱ 15 min | 🍲 35 min

This warm, comforting apple crumble features a sourdough discard topping, adding a unique twist to this classic dessert.

Ingredients:

- 1 cup sourdough discard
- 1 cup rolled oats
- 1/2 cup all-purpose flour
- 1/2 cup brown sugar
- 1/2 cup butter, melted
- 1 teaspoon cinnamon
- 6 apples, peeled and sliced

Instructions:

1. Preheat the oven to 350°F (175°C) and grease a baking dish.
2. In a bowl, mix the sourdough discard, oats, flour, brown sugar, melted butter, and cinnamon to form a crumble topping.
3. Arrange the sliced apples in the baking dish and sprinkle the crumble topping evenly over the apples.
4. Bake for 30-35 minutes until the topping is golden and the apples are tender.

8. Sourdough Discard Pumpkin Pie

👥 8 | ⏱ 15 min | 🍲 45 min

This creamy pumpkin pie features a sourdough discard crust that adds depth and flavor to this fall favorite.

Ingredients:

- 1 cup sourdough discard
- 1 1/2 cups all-purpose flour
- 1/4 cup cold butter, cubed
- 1/4 cup cold water

For the Filling:

- 2 cups pumpkin puree
- 1 cup evaporated milk
- 1/2 cup sugar
- 2 large eggs
- 1 teaspoon cinnamon
- 1/4 teaspoon nutmeg

Instructions:

1. Preheat the oven to 375°F (190°C).
2. In a bowl, mix the sourdough discard, flour, butter, and water until a dough forms. Roll out the dough and press it into a pie dish.
3. In another bowl, whisk together the pumpkin puree, evaporated milk, sugar, eggs, cinnamon, and nutmeg.
4. Pour the filling into the crust and bake for 45-50 minutes until set.

9. Sourdough Discard Shortbread Cookies

👥 24 cookies | ⏱ 10 min | 🍽 12 min

These buttery shortbread cookies are light and crumbly, with a subtle tang from the sourdough discard.

Ingredients:

- 1 cup sourdough discard
- 1 cup all-purpose flour
- 1/2 cup powdered sugar
- 1/2 cup butter, softened
- 1/4 teaspoon salt

Instructions:

1. Preheat the oven to 350°F (175°C) and line a baking sheet with parchment paper.
2. In a large bowl, cream together the butter and powdered sugar until smooth.
3. Mix in the sourdough discard.
4. Gradually add the flour and salt, mixing until a soft dough forms.

5. Roll the dough into small balls, flatten slightly, and place on the prepared baking sheet. Bake for 10-12 minutes.

10. Sourdough Discard Blueberry Muffins

👥 12 muffins | ⏱ 10 min | 🍽 25 min

These moist blueberry muffins have a light tang from the sourdough discard, making them a perfect breakfast or snack.

Ingredients:

- 1 cup sourdough discard
- 1 1/2 cups all-purpose flour
- 1/2 cup sugar
- 1/4 cup vegetable oil
- 1 large egg
- 1/2 cup milk
- 1 teaspoon vanilla extract
- 1 teaspoon baking powder
- 1/2 teaspoon baking soda
- 1/4 teaspoon salt
- 1 cup fresh or frozen blueberries

Instructions:

1. Preheat the oven to 375°F (190°C) and line a muffin tin with paper liners.
2. In a large bowl, mix the sourdough discard, flour, sugar, oil, egg, milk, and vanilla until combined.
3. Stir in the baking powder, baking soda, and salt.
4. Gently fold in the blueberries.
5. Divide the batter among the muffin cups and bake for 20-25 minutes.

11. Sourdough Discard Carrot Cake

👥 8 | ⏱ 15 min | 🍽 35 min

This moist carrot cake is spiced with cinnamon and has a hint of sourdough tang, making it a unique twist on the classic.

Ingredients:

- 1 cup sourdough discard
- 2 cups all-purpose flour
- 1/2 cup sugar
- 1/2 cup brown sugar
- 1/2 cup vegetable oil
- 3 large eggs
- 2 cups grated carrots
- 1 teaspoon cinnamon
- 1 teaspoon baking soda
- 1/4 teaspoon salt

Instructions:

1. Preheat the oven to 350°F (175°C) and grease a 9-inch round cake pan.
2. In a large bowl, mix the sourdough discard, sugar, brown sugar, oil, and eggs until smooth.
3. Stir in the grated carrots.
4. In another bowl, whisk together the flour, cinnamon, baking soda, and salt. Add to the wet ingredients and stir until just combined.
5. Pour the batter into the prepared pan and bake for 30-35 minutes.

12. Sourdough Discard Gingerbread

👥 8 | ⏱ 15 min | 🍲 35 min

This rich, spiced gingerbread is moist and flavorful, with a slight tang from the sourdough discard.

Ingredients:

- 1 cup sourdough discard
- 1 1/2 cups all-purpose flour
- 1/2 cup brown sugar
- 1/2 cup molasses
- 1/4 cup vegetable oil
- 1 large egg
- 1 teaspoon baking soda
- 1/2 teaspoon ground ginger
- 1/2 teaspoon cinnamon

- 1/4 teaspoon ground cloves
- 1/4 teaspoon salt

Instructions:

1. Preheat the oven to 350°F (175°C) and grease an 8x8-inch baking pan.
2. In a large bowl, mix the sourdough discard, brown sugar, molasses, oil, and egg until smooth.
3. In another bowl, whisk together the flour, baking soda, ginger, cinnamon, cloves, and salt.
4. Add the dry ingredients to the wet mixture and stir until just combined.
5. Pour the batter into the prepared pan and bake for 30-35 minutes.

13. Sourdough Discard Apple Pie

👥 8 | ⏱ 20 min | 🍲 50 min

This classic apple pie has a flaky sourdough discard crust that perfectly complements the sweet apple filling.

Ingredients:

- 1 cup sourdough discard
- 1 1/2 cups all-purpose flour
- 1/4 cup cold butter, cubed
- 1/4 cup cold water

For the Filling:

- 6 apples, peeled and sliced
- 1/2 cup sugar
- 1/4 cup brown sugar
- 1 teaspoon cinnamon
- 1/4 teaspoon nutmeg
- 1 tablespoon lemon juice

Instructions:

1. Preheat the oven to 375°F (190°C).
2. In a bowl, mix the sourdough discard, flour, butter, and water until a dough forms. Chill for 30 minutes.

3. In a separate bowl, mix the apples, sugars, cinnamon, nutmeg, and lemon juice.
4. Roll out the dough and line a pie dish. Add the apple mixture.
5. Roll out the remaining dough and place it over the filling. Crimp the edges and cut slits in the top.
6. Bake for 45-50 minutes until golden.

14. Sourdough Discard Chocolate Tart

👥 8 | ⏱ 20 min | 🍽 25 min

This rich chocolate tart has a sourdough discard crust that adds depth to the decadent filling.

Ingredients:

- 1 cup sourdough discard
- 1 1/2 cups all-purpose flour
- 1/4 cup cold butter, cubed
- 1/4 cup cold water

For the Filling:

- 1 cup heavy cream
- 8 oz dark chocolate, chopped
- 1 tablespoon butter
- 1 teaspoon vanilla extract

Instructions:

1. Preheat the oven to 350°F (175°C).
2. In a bowl, mix the sourdough discard, flour, butter, and water until a dough forms. Chill for 15 minutes.
3. Roll out the dough and press it into a tart pan. Bake for 15 minutes until lightly golden.
4. In a saucepan, heat the cream until simmering. Remove from heat and stir in the chocolate, butter, and vanilla until smooth.
5. Pour the filling into the crust and refrigerate until set, about 2 hours.

15. Sourdough Discard Pecan Pie

👥 8 | ⏱ 20 min | 🍽 45 min

This rich, gooey pecan pie has a sourdough discard crust, balancing the sweetness with a subtle tang.

Ingredients:

- 1 cup sourdough discard
- 1 1/2 cups all-purpose flour
- 1/4 cup cold butter, cubed
- 1/4 cup cold water

For the Filling:

- 1 cup corn syrup
- 1/2 cup brown sugar
- 3 large eggs
- 2 tablespoons melted butter
- 1 teaspoon vanilla extract
- 1 1/2 cups pecans

Instructions:

1. Preheat the oven to 350°F (175°C).
2. In a bowl, mix the sourdough discard, flour, butter, and water until a dough forms. Roll out the dough and press it into a pie dish.
3. In a separate bowl, whisk together the corn syrup, brown sugar, eggs, melted butter, and vanilla.
4. Stir in the pecans and pour the filling into the crust.
5. Bake for 40-45 minutes until set.

16. Sourdough Discard Cinnamon Sugar Donuts

👥 12 donuts | ⏱ 15 min | 🍽 15 min

These soft, fluffy donuts are coated in cinnamon sugar and have a slight tang from the sourdough discard.

Ingredients:

- 1 cup sourdough discard
- 2 cups all-purpose flour
- 1/2 cup sugar
- 1/4 cup butter, melted
- 1/2 cup milk
- 1 large egg
- 1 teaspoon baking powder
- 1/2 teaspoon baking soda
- 1/4 teaspoon salt

For the Coating:

- 1/2 cup sugar
- 1 teaspoon cinnamon

Instructions:

1. Preheat the oven to 375°F (190°C) and grease a donut pan.
2. In a large bowl, mix the sourdough discard, flour, sugar, melted butter, milk, egg, baking powder, baking soda, and salt until a smooth batter forms.
3. Spoon the batter into the donut pan and bake for 12-15 minutes until golden.
4. In a separate bowl, mix the sugar and cinnamon. Once the donuts are cool, dip them in the cinnamon sugar.

17. Sourdough Discard Chocolate Chip Scones

👥 8 scones | ⏲ 15 min | 🍲 20 min

These tender scones are packed with chocolate chips, with a slight tang from the sourdough discard.

Ingredients:

- 1 cup sourdough discard
- 2 cups all-purpose flour
- 1/4 cup sugar
- 1/2 cup cold butter, cubed
- 1/2 cup chocolate chips
- 1/2 cup heavy cream

- 1 large egg
- 1 teaspoon vanilla extract
- 1 teaspoon baking powder
- 1/2 teaspoon salt

Instructions:

1. Preheat the oven to 400°F (200°C) and line a baking sheet with parchment paper.
2. In a large bowl, mix the flour, sugar, baking powder, and salt. Cut in the cold butter until the mixture resembles coarse crumbs.
3. Stir in the sourdough discard, heavy cream, egg, vanilla, and chocolate chips.
4. Drop the dough onto the baking sheet in 8 mounds and bake for 15-20 minutes until golden.

18. Sourdough Discard Oatmeal Raisin Cookies

👥 24 cookies | ⏲ 15 min | 🍲 12 min

These chewy oatmeal raisin cookies have a slight tang from the sourdough discard and are packed with wholesome oats and raisins.

Ingredients:

- 1/2 cup sourdough discard
- 1 1/2 cups rolled oats
- 1 cup all-purpose flour
- 1/2 cup butter, softened
- 1/2 cup brown sugar
- 1/4 cup white sugar
- 1 large egg
- 1 teaspoon vanilla extract
- 1/2 teaspoon baking soda
- 1/4 teaspoon salt
- 1/2 cup raisins

Instructions:

1. Preheat the oven to 350°F (175°C) and line a baking sheet with parchment paper.
2. In a large bowl, cream together the butter, brown sugar, and white sugar.

3. Mix in the sourdough discard, egg, and vanilla.
4. In another bowl, whisk together the oats, flour, baking soda, and salt. Add to the wet ingredients and stir until combined.
5. Stir in the raisins and drop spoonfuls of dough onto the prepared baking sheet. Bake for 10-12 minutes.

19. Sourdough Discard Lemon Poppy Seed Muffins

👥 12 muffins | ⏱ 10 min | 🍽 25 min

These light and tangy muffins are packed with lemon flavor and crunchy poppy seeds, with a hint of sourdough tang.

Ingredients:

- 1 cup sourdough discard
- 1 1/2 cups all-purpose flour
- 1/2 cup sugar
- 1/4 cup vegetable oil
- 1 large egg
- 1/2 cup milk
- 1 teaspoon vanilla extract
- 1 tablespoon lemon zest
- 1 teaspoon baking powder
- 1/2 teaspoon baking soda
- 1/4 teaspoon salt
- 1 tablespoon poppy seeds

Instructions:

1. Preheat the oven to 375°F (190°C) and line a muffin tin with paper liners.
2. In a large bowl, mix the sourdough discard, flour, sugar, oil, egg, milk, vanilla, and lemon zest until combined.
3. Stir in the baking powder, baking soda, salt, and poppy seeds.
4. Divide the batter among the muffin cups and bake for 20-25 minutes.

20. Sourdough Discard Vanilla Cupcakes

👥 12 cupcakes | ⏱ 15 min | 🍽 20 min

These classic vanilla cupcakes are soft, fluffy, and have a slight tang from the sourdough discard, making them a perfect base for any frosting.

Ingredients:

- 1 cup sourdough discard
- 1 1/2 cups all-purpose flour
- 1/2 cup sugar
- 1/2 cup butter, softened
- 2 large eggs
- 1/2 cup milk
- 1 teaspoon vanilla extract
- 1 teaspoon baking powder
- 1/4 teaspoon salt

Instructions:

1. Preheat the oven to 350°F (175°C) and line a muffin tin with paper liners.
2. In a large bowl, cream together the butter and sugar until light and fluffy.
3. Mix in the sourdough discard, eggs, milk, and vanilla extract.
4. In another bowl, whisk together the flour, baking powder, and salt. Add to the wet ingredients and stir until just combined.
5. Divide the batter among the muffin cups and bake for 18-20 minutes until golden.

21. Sourdough Discard Lemon Bars

👥 12 bars | ⏱ 15 min | 🍽 25 min

Tangy and sweet lemon bars with a buttery crust and a touch of sourdough discard for added depth of flavor.

Ingredients:

- 1 cup sourdough discard

- 1 1/2 cups all-purpose flour
- 1/2 cup powdered sugar
- 1/2 cup butter, melted
- 4 large eggs
- 1 1/2 cups granulated sugar
- 1/2 cup lemon juice
- 1/2 teaspoon baking powder

Instructions:

1. Preheat the oven to 350°F (175°C) and grease a 9x13-inch baking dish.
2. In a bowl, mix sourdough discard, flour, powdered sugar, and melted butter. Press into the bottom of the baking dish.
3. Bake the crust for 10-12 minutes until lightly golden.
4. In another bowl, whisk together eggs, granulated sugar, lemon juice, and baking powder. Pour over the baked crust.
5. Bake for another 20-25 minutes until set. Let cool before cutting into bars.

22. Sourdough Discard Chocolate Cake

👥 8 | ⏱ 15 min | 🍲 30 min

Rich and moist chocolate cake with a subtle sourdough tang, perfect for any special occasion.

Ingredients:

- 1 cup sourdough discard
- 1 1/2 cups all-purpose flour
- 1/2 cup cocoa powder
- 1 teaspoon baking soda
- 1/2 teaspoon baking powder
- 1/4 teaspoon salt
- 1 cup granulated sugar
- 1/2 cup vegetable oil
- 2 large eggs
- 1 cup buttermilk
- 1 teaspoon vanilla extract

Instructions:

1. Preheat the oven to 350°F (175°C) and grease a 9-inch round cake pan.
2. In a large bowl, whisk together the flour, cocoa powder, baking soda, baking powder, and salt.
3. In another bowl, mix the sourdough discard, sugar, oil, eggs, buttermilk, and vanilla.
4. Combine the wet and dry ingredients and pour the batter into the prepared pan.
5. Bake for 25-30 minutes or until a toothpick comes out clean. Let cool before frosting or serving.

23. Sourdough Discard Cinnamon Rolls

👥 12 rolls | ⏱ 20 min | 🍲 25 min

Soft and gooey cinnamon rolls with a sourdough discard dough and a sweet cinnamon sugar filling.

Ingredients:

- 1 cup sourdough discard
- 3 cups all-purpose flour
- 1/4 cup granulated sugar
- 1/2 teaspoon salt
- 1/4 cup butter, melted
- 1/2 cup warm milk
- 1 large egg
- 1 teaspoon instant yeast

For the Filling:

- 1/4 cup butter, softened
- 1/2 cup brown sugar
- 1 tablespoon cinnamon

Instructions:

1. In a bowl, mix sourdough discard, flour, sugar, salt, butter, milk, egg, and yeast until a dough forms. Knead for 8-10 minutes until smooth. Let rise for 1 hour.

2. Roll out the dough into a rectangle and spread with softened butter. Sprinkle with brown sugar and cinnamon.
3. Roll the dough into a log and slice into 12 rolls. Place in a greased baking dish and let rise for another 30 minutes.
4. Preheat the oven to 350°F (175°C) and bake for 20-25 minutes until golden brown. Frost if desired.

24. Sourdough Discard Chocolate Chip Cookies

👥 24 cookies | ⏱ 10 min | 🍽 12 min

Crispy on the outside and chewy in the center, these chocolate chip cookies get a unique twist from sourdough discard.

Ingredients:

- 1/2 cup sourdough discard
- 1 1/2 cups all-purpose flour
- 1/2 cup unsalted butter, softened
- 1/2 cup granulated sugar
- 1/2 cup brown sugar
- 1 large egg
- 1 teaspoon vanilla extract
- 1/2 teaspoon baking soda
- 1/4 teaspoon salt
- 1 cup chocolate chips

Instructions:

1. Preheat the oven to 350°F (175°C) and line a baking sheet with parchment paper.
2. In a large bowl, cream together the butter, granulated sugar, and brown sugar until light and fluffy.
3. Mix in the egg, sourdough discard, and vanilla extract.
4. Stir in the flour, baking soda, and salt until combined, then fold in the chocolate chips.
5. Drop spoonfuls of dough onto the baking sheet and bake for 10-12 minutes until golden around the edges.

25. Sourdough Discard Brownies

👥 12 brownies | ⏱ 10 min | 🍽 25 min

Rich, fudgy brownies with a subtle tang from sourdough discard.

Ingredients:

- 1/2 cup sourdough discard
- 1/2 cup butter, melted
- 1 cup granulated sugar
- 1/2 cup cocoa powder
- 1/4 cup all-purpose flour
- 1/2 teaspoon baking powder
- 2 large eggs
- 1 teaspoon vanilla extract
- 1/4 teaspoon salt

Instructions:

1. Preheat the oven to 350°F (175°C) and grease an 8x8-inch baking dish.
2. In a large bowl, whisk together the butter, sugar, cocoa powder, and sourdough discard.
3. Stir in the eggs and vanilla extract.
4. Add the flour, baking powder, and salt, and mix until combined.
5. Pour the batter into the prepared pan and bake for 20-25 minutes until set. Let cool before slicing.

26. Sourdough Discard Blueberry Muffins

👥 12 muffins | ⏱ 10 min | 🍽 20 min

Soft and fluffy muffins bursting with fresh blueberries and a hint of sourdough.

Ingredients:

- 1 cup sourdough discard
- 1 1/2 cups all-purpose flour
- 1/2 cup granulated sugar
- 1/4 cup vegetable oil

- 1/2 cup milk
- 1 large egg
- 1 teaspoon baking powder
- 1/4 teaspoon salt
- 1 cup fresh or frozen blueberries

Instructions:

1. Preheat the oven to 375°F (190°C) and line a muffin tin with paper liners.
2. In a large bowl, mix together the sourdough discard, sugar, oil, milk, and egg.
3. In another bowl, whisk together the flour, baking powder, and salt. Add the dry ingredients to the wet and mix until just combined.
4. Fold in the blueberries.
5. Divide the batter evenly among the muffin cups and bake for 18-20 minutes until golden brown.

27. Sourdough Discard Carrot Cake

👥 8 | ⏱ 15 min | 🍜 30 min

A moist and flavorful carrot cake with sourdough discard, topped with a rich cream cheese frosting.

Ingredients:

- 1 cup sourdough discard
- 1 1/2 cups all-purpose flour
- 1/2 cup granulated sugar
- 1/2 cup brown sugar
- 1/2 cup vegetable oil
- 2 large eggs
- 1 teaspoon vanilla extract
- 1 teaspoon baking soda
- 1/2 teaspoon cinnamon
- 1/4 teaspoon nutmeg
- 1/4 teaspoon salt
- 1 cup grated carrots

For the Frosting:

- 8 oz cream cheese, softened
- 1/4 cup butter, softened
- 1 cup powdered sugar
- 1 teaspoon vanilla extract

Instructions:

1. Preheat the oven to 350°F (175°C) and grease a 9-inch round cake pan.
2. In a bowl, mix the sourdough discard, sugars, oil, eggs, and vanilla.
3. In another bowl, whisk together flour, baking soda, cinnamon, nutmeg, and salt. Combine with the wet ingredients and stir in the grated carrots.
4. Pour the batter into the prepared pan and bake for 25-30 minutes.
5. For the frosting, beat together the cream cheese, butter, powdered sugar, and vanilla until smooth. Spread on the cooled cake.

28. Sourdough Discard Banana Bread

👥 8 | ⏱ 10 min | 🍜 1 hr

A classic banana bread with the added depth of sourdough discard.

Ingredients:

- 1 cup sourdough discard
- 1 1/2 cups all-purpose flour
- 1/2 cup granulated sugar
- 1/4 cup melted butter
- 1 teaspoon vanilla extract
- 2 large ripe bananas, mashed
- 1 large egg
- 1 teaspoon baking soda
- 1/4 teaspoon salt

Instructions:

1. Preheat the oven to 350°F (175°C) and grease a loaf pan.

2. In a large bowl, mix together the sourdough discard, sugar, melted butter, vanilla, bananas, and egg.
3. In another bowl, whisk together the flour, baking soda, and salt. Add the dry ingredients to the wet and stir until just combined.
4. Pour the batter into the loaf pan and bake for 50-60 minutes, or until a toothpick inserted in the center comes out clean.

29. Sourdough Discard Pumpkin Pie

👥 8 | ⏱ 15 min | 🍽 50 min

A rich and creamy pumpkin pie with a sourdough discard crust.

Ingredients:

- 1 cup sourdough discard
- 1 1/2 cups all-purpose flour
- 1/2 cup cold butter, cubed
- 1/4 cup cold water
- 2 cups pumpkin puree
- 1/2 cup brown sugar
- 1/2 cup heavy cream
- 2 large eggs
- 1 teaspoon cinnamon
- 1/2 teaspoon nutmeg
- 1/4 teaspoon cloves

Instructions:

1. Preheat the oven to 350°F (175°C).
2. In a bowl, mix sourdough discard, flour, and cold butter until crumbly. Add cold

water and form a dough. Roll out and press into a pie dish.
3. In another bowl, mix pumpkin puree, brown sugar, cream, eggs, cinnamon, nutmeg, and cloves. Pour into the pie crust.
4. Bake for 45-50 minutes until set. Let cool before serving.

30. Sourdough Discard Chocolate Truffles

👥 12 truffles | ⏱ 15 min | 🍽 N/A (chilling time)

Rich and decadent chocolate truffles with a sourdough discard base.

Ingredients:

- 1/4 cup sourdough discard
- 8 oz dark chocolate, chopped
- 1/2 cup heavy cream
- 1 tablespoon butter
- 1 teaspoon vanilla extract
- Cocoa powder for rolling

Instructions:

1. In a small saucepan, heat the cream and butter until just simmering. Remove from heat and stir in the chocolate until melted.
2. Stir in the sourdough discard and vanilla extract.
3. Pour the mixture into a bowl and refrigerate for 2 hours until firm.
4. Scoop small amounts of the chocolate mixture and roll into balls. Roll each truffle in cocoa powder to coat.

Chapter 8: Special Treats & Festive Bakes

1. Sourdough Discard Gingerbread Cookies

👥 24 cookies | ⏱ 15 min | 🍲 12 min

These classic gingerbread cookies are soft, spiced, and perfect for the holiday season. The sourdough discard adds an extra depth of flavor.

Ingredients:

- 1 cup sourdough discard
- 3 cups all-purpose flour
- 1/2 cup brown sugar
- 1/2 cup molasses
- 1/2 cup butter, softened
- 1 large egg
- 1 teaspoon baking soda
- 1 teaspoon ground ginger
- 1 teaspoon cinnamon
- 1/4 teaspoon ground cloves
- 1/4 teaspoon salt

Instructions:

1. Preheat the oven to 350°F (175°C) and line a baking sheet with parchment paper.
2. In a large bowl, cream together the butter and brown sugar until light and fluffy.
3. Mix in the sourdough discard, molasses, and egg.
4. In another bowl, whisk together the flour, baking soda, ginger, cinnamon, cloves, and salt. Gradually add to the wet ingredients and mix until combined.
5. Roll out the dough on a floured surface and cut into shapes using cookie cutters.
6. Place the cookies on the prepared baking sheet and bake for 10-12 minutes until golden.

2. Sourdough Discard Fruitcake

👥 8 | ⏱ 20 min | 🍲 1 hr

This rich and moist fruitcake is filled with dried fruits and nuts, perfect for the holiday season. The sourdough discard adds a slight tang to balance the sweetness.

Ingredients:

- 1 cup sourdough discard
- 2 cups all-purpose flour
- 1/2 cup brown sugar
- 1/2 cup butter, softened
- 3 large eggs
- 1 teaspoon vanilla extract
- 1 teaspoon baking powder
- 1/2 teaspoon cinnamon
- 1/4 teaspoon nutmeg
- 1/4 teaspoon allspice
- 1/2 cup mixed dried fruits (raisins, currants, apricots, etc.)
- 1/2 cup chopped nuts (walnuts, pecans, etc.)

Instructions:

1. Preheat the oven to 325°F (160°C) and grease a loaf pan.
2. In a large bowl, cream together the butter and brown sugar until light and fluffy.
3. Mix in the sourdough discard, eggs, and vanilla extract.
4. In another bowl, whisk together the flour, baking powder, cinnamon, nutmeg, and allspice. Gradually add to the wet ingredients and stir until combined.
5. Fold in the dried fruits and nuts.
6. Pour the batter into the loaf pan and bake for 60-70 minutes, or until a toothpick comes out clean.

3. Sourdough Discard Stollen

👥 8 | ⏱ 30 min (+ rise) | 🍲 40 min

This traditional German Christmas bread is filled with dried fruit, marzipan, and spices, with a sourdough discard dough that gives it a unique twist.

Ingredients:

- 1 cup sourdough discard
- 3 cups all-purpose flour
- 1/4 cup sugar
- 1/2 cup warm milk
- 1/4 cup butter, melted
- 1 large egg
- 1 teaspoon instant yeast
- 1/2 teaspoon cinnamon
- 1/4 teaspoon nutmeg
- 1/4 teaspoon salt
- 1/2 cup mixed dried fruits (raisins, currants, etc.)
- 1/4 cup chopped almonds
- 1/4 cup marzipan (optional)
- Powdered sugar for dusting

Instructions:

1. In a large bowl, mix the sourdough discard, flour, sugar, warm milk, melted butter, egg, yeast, cinnamon, nutmeg, and salt. Stir until a soft dough forms.
2. Knead the dough for 8-10 minutes until smooth and elastic. Let rise in a greased bowl for 1-2 hours until doubled in size.
3. Roll out the dough into a rectangle. If using marzipan, roll it into a log and place it in the center of the dough. Fold the dough over and seal the edges.
4. Place the loaf on a greased baking sheet and let rise for another 30 minutes.
5. Preheat the oven to 350°F (175°C) and bake for 35-40 minutes until golden.
6. Once cool, dust generously with powdered sugar.

4. Sourdough Discard Panettone

👥 10 | ⏱ 30 min (+ rise) | 🍲 45 min

This Italian Christmas bread is fluffy and rich, filled with candied fruit and raisins, and made even better with sourdough discard.

Ingredients:

- 1 cup sourdough discard
- 4 cups all-purpose flour
- 1/2 cup sugar
- 1/2 cup warm milk
- 1/4 cup butter, melted
- 2 large eggs
- 2 teaspoons instant yeast
- 1 teaspoon vanilla extract
- 1/2 teaspoon salt
- 1/2 cup candied fruit
- 1/2 cup raisins
- 1/4 cup chopped almonds

Instructions:

1. In a large bowl, mix the sourdough discard, flour, sugar, warm milk, melted butter, eggs, yeast, vanilla, and salt. Stir until a soft dough forms.
2. Knead the dough for about 10 minutes until smooth and elastic. Let rise for 2 hours.
3. Add the candied fruit, raisins, and almonds, and knead until evenly distributed.
4. Transfer the dough to a panettone mold or a tall greased baking pan and let rise for another hour.
5. Preheat the oven to 350°F (175°C) and bake for 40-45 minutes until golden brown.

5. Sourdough Discard Yule Log (Bûche de Noël)

👥 8 | ⏱ 30 min | 🍮 20 min

This festive Yule log cake is light, filled with a rich cream, and rolled to resemble a log. The sourdough discard adds a delicate depth of flavor.

Ingredients:

- 1/2 cup sourdough discard
- 1/2 cup all-purpose flour
- 1/4 cup cocoa powder
- 4 large eggs
- 1/2 cup sugar
- 1 teaspoon vanilla extract
- 1 teaspoon baking powder
- 1/4 teaspoon salt

For the Filling:

- 1 cup heavy cream
- 1/4 cup powdered sugar
- 1 teaspoon vanilla extract

For the Frosting:

- 1/2 cup butter, softened
- 1 cup powdered sugar
- 1/4 cup cocoa powder
- 1 tablespoon milk

Instructions:

1. Preheat the oven to 350°F (175°C) and line a baking sheet with parchment paper.
2. In a large bowl, whisk the eggs and sugar until light and fluffy. Stir in the sourdough discard and vanilla extract.
3. In another bowl, whisk together the flour, cocoa powder, baking powder, and salt. Gently fold into the wet ingredients.
4. Pour the batter onto the prepared baking sheet and spread evenly. Bake for 10-12 minutes.
5. Immediately roll the cake in a clean towel and let cool.
6. For the filling, whip the cream with powdered sugar and vanilla until stiff peaks form.
7. Unroll the cake, spread the filling, and roll it back up.
8. For the frosting, beat the butter, powdered sugar, cocoa, and milk until smooth. Frost the outside of the cake to resemble a log.

6. Sourdough Discard Hot Cross Buns

👥 12 buns | ⏱ 20 min (+ rise) | 🍮 25 min

These traditional spiced buns are soft, fluffy, and marked with a cross on top. The sourdough discard gives them an extra layer of flavor.

Ingredients:

- 1 cup sourdough discard
- 3 cups all-purpose flour
- 1/2 cup warm milk
- 1/4 cup sugar
- 1/4 cup butter, melted
- 1 large egg
- 1 teaspoon instant yeast
- 1/2 teaspoon cinnamon
- 1/4 teaspoon nutmeg
- 1/4 teaspoon allspice
- 1/2 cup raisins or currants
- 1/4 teaspoon salt

For the Cross:

- 1/4 cup all-purpose flour
- 2 tablespoons water

For the Glaze:

- 1/4 cup apricot jam, melted

Instructions:

1. In a large bowl, mix the sourdough discard, flour, milk, sugar, melted butter, egg, yeast, cinnamon, nutmeg, allspice, and salt. Stir until a soft dough forms.
2. Knead the dough for about 10 minutes until smooth and elastic. Let rise for 1-2 hours until doubled in size.
3. Preheat the oven to 350°F (175°C).
4. Shape the dough into 12 buns and place on a greased baking sheet. Let rise for another 30 minutes.
5. Mix the flour and water to make a thick paste and pipe a cross onto each bun.
6. Bake for 20-25 minutes until golden.
7. Brush the buns with the melted apricot jam for a shiny finish.

7. Sourdough Discard Pecan Tassies

👥 24 tassies | ⏱ 15 min | 🍽 25 min

These mini pecan pies are made with a sourdough discard crust and a rich, sweet pecan filling. Perfect for parties or holiday gatherings.

Ingredients:

- 1 cup sourdough discard
- 2 cups all-purpose flour
- 1/2 cup butter, softened
- 1/4 cup cream cheese

For the Filling:

- 1 cup pecans, chopped
- 1/2 cup brown sugar
- 1 large egg
- 1 tablespoon butter, melted
- 1 teaspoon vanilla extract

Instructions:

1. Preheat the oven to 350°F (175°C) and grease a mini muffin tin.

2. In a large bowl, mix the sourdough discard, flour, butter, and cream cheese until a dough forms.
3. Roll the dough into small balls and press into the muffin tin to form mini crusts.
4. In another bowl, whisk together the chopped pecans, brown sugar, egg, melted butter, and vanilla.
5. Spoon the filling into each crust and bake for 20-25 minutes until golden and set.

8. Sourdough Discard Pumpkin Roll

👥 8 | ⏱ 20 min | 🍽 15 min

This light and spongy pumpkin roll is filled with a rich cream cheese filling, with the sourdough discard adding depth to the flavor.

Ingredients:

- 1/2 cup sourdough discard
- 3/4 cup all-purpose flour
- 1/2 cup pumpkin puree
- 3 large eggs
- 1/2 cup sugar
- 1 teaspoon baking powder
- 1/2 teaspoon cinnamon
- 1/4 teaspoon nutmeg
- 1/4 teaspoon salt

For the Filling:

- 1/2 cup cream cheese, softened
- 1/4 cup butter, softened
- 1/2 cup powdered sugar
- 1 teaspoon vanilla extract

Instructions:

1. Preheat the oven to 350°F (175°C) and line a baking sheet with parchment paper.
2. In a large bowl, whisk the eggs and sugar until light and fluffy. Stir in the sourdough discard and pumpkin puree.

3. In another bowl, whisk together the flour, baking powder, cinnamon, nutmeg, and salt. Fold into the wet ingredients.
4. Pour the batter onto the prepared baking sheet and bake for 10–12 minutes.
5. Roll the cake in a clean towel and let cool.
6. For the filling, beat the cream cheese, butter, powdered sugar, and vanilla until smooth. Spread the filling over the unrolled cake and roll it back up.

9. Sourdough Discard Christmas Pudding

👥 8 | ⏱ 30 min | 🍮 2 hr

This traditional Christmas pudding is dense, rich, and filled with dried fruits and spices. The sourdough discard adds a slight tang to balance the sweetness.

Ingredients:

- 1 cup sourdough discard
- 1 1/2 cups all-purpose flour
- 1/2 cup brown sugar
- 1/2 cup butter, softened
- 3 large eggs
- 1/2 cup breadcrumbs
- 1 teaspoon cinnamon
- 1/2 teaspoon nutmeg
- 1/4 teaspoon ground cloves
- 1/2 cup raisins
- 1/2 cup currants
- 1/4 cup chopped dried apricots
- 1/4 cup chopped nuts (optional)
- 1/2 cup dark rum (optional)

Instructions:

1. Grease a 1.5-liter pudding basin.
2. In a large bowl, cream together the butter and sugar until light and fluffy. Add the sourdough discard and eggs, mixing until smooth.

3. Stir in the flour, breadcrumbs, cinnamon, nutmeg, and cloves. Fold in the dried fruit and nuts, and add the rum if using.
4. Spoon the mixture into the pudding basin and cover tightly with foil.
5. Steam the pudding for 2 hours, checking occasionally to ensure there is enough water in the pot.
6. Let the pudding cool and serve with brandy butter or custard.

10. Sourdough Discard Chocolate Babka

👥 8 | ⏱ 30 min (+ rise) | 🍮 35 min

This sweet, chocolate-filled babka is perfect for special occasions. The sourdough discard gives the dough an extra depth of flavor.

Ingredients:

- 1 cup sourdough discard
- 3 cups all-purpose flour
- 1/4 cup sugar
- 1/2 cup warm milk
- 1/4 cup butter, melted
- 2 large eggs
- 1 teaspoon instant yeast
- 1/2 teaspoon salt

For the Filling:

- 1/2 cup chocolate spread (or Nutella)
- 1/4 cup chopped dark chocolate
- 1/4 cup chopped nuts (optional)

Instructions:

1. In a large bowl, mix the sourdough discard, flour, sugar, warm milk, melted butter, eggs, yeast, and salt until a dough forms.
2. Knead for about 10 minutes until smooth and elastic. Let rise for 1-2 hours.
3. Roll out the dough into a large rectangle. Spread the chocolate filling evenly over

the dough and sprinkle with chocolate chunks and nuts.

4. Roll the dough tightly into a log, then slice the log in half lengthwise. Twist the two pieces together and place in a greased loaf pan.
5. Let rise for another 30 minutes. Preheat the oven to 350°F (175°C).
6. Bake for 30-35 minutes until golden and cooked through.

11. Sourdough Discard Sticky Toffee Pudding

👥 8 | ⏲ 20 min | 🍳 30 min

This indulgent sticky toffee pudding is moist and rich, with a sourdough discard base that adds a unique twist to the classic British dessert.

Ingredients:

- 1 cup sourdough discard
- 1 cup all-purpose flour
- 1/2 cup butter, softened
- 1/2 cup brown sugar
- 2 large eggs
- 1 teaspoon vanilla extract
- 1 teaspoon baking powder
- 1/2 cup dates, chopped
- 1/2 cup hot water

For the Toffee Sauce:

- 1/2 cup butter
- 1/2 cup brown sugar
- 1/2 cup heavy cream
- 1 teaspoon vanilla extract

Instructions:

1. Preheat the oven to 350°F (175°C) and grease a baking dish.
2. In a small bowl, soak the chopped dates in the hot water for 10 minutes to soften.
3. In a large bowl, cream together the butter and brown sugar. Add the eggs, vanilla,

and sourdough discard, mixing until smooth.

4. Stir in the flour and baking powder, then fold in the soaked dates and their water.
5. Pour the batter into the prepared dish and bake for 25-30 minutes.
6. While the pudding bakes, make the toffee sauce by melting the butter and brown sugar in a saucepan. Stir in the cream and vanilla, and simmer until thickened.
7. Once the pudding is done, pour the toffee sauce over the top and serve warm.

12. Sourdough Discard Almond Biscotti

👥 24 biscotti | ⏲ 15 min | 🍳 40 min

These crunchy almond biscotti are perfect for dipping in coffee or hot chocolate, and the sourdough discard gives them a slightly tangy flavor.

Ingredients:

- 1 cup sourdough discard
- 2 cups all-purpose flour
- 1/2 cup sugar
- 1/4 cup butter, softened
- 2 large eggs
- 1 teaspoon vanilla extract
- 1 teaspoon baking powder
- 1/4 teaspoon salt
- 1 cup sliced almonds

Instructions:

1. Preheat the oven to 350°F (175°C) and line a baking sheet with parchment paper.
2. In a large bowl, cream together the butter and sugar until light and fluffy. Mix in the sourdough discard, eggs, and vanilla extract.
3. In another bowl, whisk together the flour, baking powder, and salt. Gradually add to the wet ingredients.
4. Fold in the sliced almonds.

5. Divide the dough in half and shape each portion into a log. Place the logs on the baking sheet and flatten slightly.
6. Bake for 25-30 minutes until golden. Let cool for 10 minutes, then slice into 1/2-inch thick pieces.
7. Return the biscotti to the baking sheet and bake for another 10 minutes, flipping halfway through.

13. Sourdough Discard Chocolate Truffles

👥 12 truffles | ⏱ 15 min | 🍲 5 min (chilling)

These rich and decadent chocolate truffles are made with sourdough discard, giving them a subtle tang that balances the sweetness of the chocolate.

Ingredients:

- 1/4 cup sourdough discard
- 8 oz dark chocolate, chopped
- 1/2 cup heavy cream
- 1 tablespoon butter
- 1 teaspoon vanilla extract
- Cocoa powder for rolling

Instructions:

1. In a small saucepan, heat the cream and butter over medium heat until just simmering. Remove from heat and stir in the chocolate until melted and smooth.
2. Stir in the sourdough discard and vanilla extract until well combined.
3. Pour the mixture into a bowl and refrigerate for 2 hours or until firm.
4. Scoop small amounts of the chocolate mixture and roll into balls. Roll each truffle in cocoa powder to coat.
5. Store in the refrigerator until ready to serve.

14. Sourdough Discard Pecan Pie Bars

👥 16 bars | ⏱ 20 min | 🍲 40 min

These pecan pie bars are perfect for sharing at festive gatherings. The sourdough discard gives the crust a flaky, buttery texture.

Ingredients:

- 1 cup sourdough discard
- 1 1/2 cups all-purpose flour
- 1/4 cup butter, cold and cubed
- 1/4 cup brown sugar

For the Filling:

- 1 cup pecans, chopped
- 1/2 cup brown sugar
- 1/4 cup corn syrup
- 2 large eggs
- 1 tablespoon melted butter
- 1 teaspoon vanilla extract

Instructions:

1. Preheat the oven to 350°F (175°C) and line an 8x8-inch baking dish with parchment paper.
2. In a large bowl, mix the sourdough discard, flour, butter, and brown sugar until a crumbly dough forms. Press into the bottom of the baking dish and bake for 10 minutes.
3. In another bowl, whisk together the pecans, brown sugar, corn syrup, eggs, melted butter, and vanilla. Pour the filling over the pre-baked crust.
4. Bake for 30-35 minutes until the filling is set.
5. Let cool before cutting into bars.

15. Sourdough Discard Linzer Cookies

👥 24 cookies | ⏱ 20 min | 🍽 12 min

These delicate Linzer cookies are filled with raspberry jam and have a tender, crumbly sourdough discard base.

Ingredients:

- 1 cup sourdough discard
- 2 cups all-purpose flour
- 1/2 cup butter, softened
- 1/2 cup powdered sugar
- 1 large egg
- 1 teaspoon vanilla extract
- 1/2 teaspoon baking powder
- 1/4 teaspoon salt
- Raspberry jam for filling
- Powdered sugar for dusting

Instructions:

1. Preheat the oven to 350°F (175°C) and line a baking sheet with parchment paper.
2. In a large bowl, cream together the butter and powdered sugar until light and fluffy. Mix in the sourdough discard, egg, and vanilla extract.
3. In another bowl, whisk together the flour, baking powder, and salt. Gradually add to the wet ingredients and mix until combined.
4. Roll out the dough on a floured surface and cut into shapes with a cookie cutter. Cut out a small circle in the center of half of the cookies.
5. Bake for 10-12 minutes until lightly golden.
6. Once cool, spread raspberry jam on the solid cookies and sandwich with the cut-out cookies. Dust with powdered sugar.

16. Sourdough Discard Tiramisu

👥 8 | ⏱ 30 min | 🍽 4 hr (chilling)

This twist on the classic Italian dessert uses sourdough discard in the ladyfinger layers, adding a slight tang to balance the sweetness of the mascarpone cream.

Ingredients:

- 1 cup sourdough discard
- 1 1/2 cups all-purpose flour
- 1/2 cup sugar
- 4 large eggs
- 1/2 teaspoon baking powder
- 1/4 teaspoon salt

For the Filling:

- 1 cup mascarpone cheese
- 1 cup heavy cream
- 1/4 cup powdered sugar
- 1 teaspoon vanilla extract
- 1 cup brewed espresso, cooled
- Cocoa powder for dusting

Instructions:

1. Preheat the oven to 350°F (175°C) and line a baking sheet with parchment paper.
2. In a large bowl, beat the eggs and sugar until light and fluffy. Stir in the sourdough discard.
3. In another bowl, whisk together the flour, baking powder, and salt. Gently fold into the wet ingredients.
4. Pour the batter onto the prepared baking sheet and bake for 10-12 minutes.
5. Once cool, cut the sponge cake into rectangles to resemble ladyfingers.
6. In a separate bowl, whisk together the mascarpone, heavy cream, powdered sugar, and vanilla until smooth.
7. Dip each ladyfinger in the espresso and layer in a dish with the mascarpone mixture.
8. Chill for at least 4 hours and dust with cocoa powder before serving.

17. Sourdough Discard Chocolate Eclairs

👥 **12 eclairs** | ⏱ **30 min** | 🍳 **25 min**

These light, airy chocolate eclairs are filled with a rich pastry cream and topped with chocolate glaze. The sourdough discard adds extra structure to the choux pastry.

Ingredients:

- 1 cup sourdough discard
- 1 cup all-purpose flour
- 1/2 cup water
- 1/2 cup butter
- 4 large eggs

For the Filling:

- 1 cup milk
- 1/4 cup sugar
- 2 large egg yolks
- 1 tablespoon cornstarch
- 1 teaspoon vanilla extract

For the Glaze:

- 1/2 cup dark chocolate, melted
- 1/4 cup heavy cream

Instructions:

1. Preheat the oven to 400°F (200°C) and line a baking sheet with parchment paper.
2. In a saucepan, heat the water and butter until boiling. Remove from heat and stir in the flour and sourdough discard until smooth.
3. Return to heat and cook for 1-2 minutes, stirring constantly.
4. Remove from heat and beat in the eggs one at a time until smooth and glossy.
5. Pipe the dough onto the prepared baking sheet in 4-inch long strips and bake for 20-25 minutes until golden and puffed.
6. For the filling, heat the milk in a saucepan. In a bowl, whisk the egg yolks, sugar, and cornstarch. Slowly pour the hot milk into the egg mixture, then return to the saucepan and cook until thickened. Stir in the vanilla.
7. Once the eclairs are cool, fill them with the pastry cream.
8. For the glaze, heat the chocolate and cream together until smooth. Dip the tops of the eclairs in the glaze.

18. Sourdough Discard Italian Panforte

👥 **8** | ⏱ **20 min** | 🍳 **35 min**

This chewy, dense Italian fruitcake is packed with nuts, dried fruit, and spices, with a touch of sourdough discard for a unique flavor.

Ingredients:

- 1 cup sourdough discard
- 1 cup all-purpose flour
- 1/2 cup sugar
- 1/4 cup honey
- 1/4 cup butter, melted
- 1/2 cup chopped almonds
- 1/2 cup chopped hazelnuts
- 1/2 cup dried figs, chopped
- 1/4 cup dried apricots, chopped
- 1/4 cup candied orange peel, chopped
- 1/2 teaspoon cinnamon
- 1/4 teaspoon nutmeg

Instructions:

1. Preheat the oven to 325°F (160°C) and line a round cake pan with parchment paper.
2. In a large bowl, mix the sourdough discard, flour, sugar, honey, melted butter, almonds, hazelnuts, figs, apricots, orange peel, cinnamon, and nutmeg until well combined.
3. Press the mixture into the prepared pan and bake for 30-35 minutes until set and golden.
4. Let cool completely before slicing into wedges.

19. Sourdough Discard Pumpkin Cheesecake

👥 8 | ⏱ 30 min | 🍲 1 hr

This creamy pumpkin cheesecake has a sourdough discard crust that adds an extra dimension to the rich filling.

Ingredients:

- 1 cup sourdough discard
- 1 1/2 cups all-purpose flour
- 1/4 cup butter, cold and cubed
- 1/4 cup sugar

For the Filling:

- 1 cup pumpkin puree
- 2 cups cream cheese, softened
- 1/2 cup sugar
- 2 large eggs
- 1 teaspoon vanilla extract
- 1/2 teaspoon cinnamon
- 1/4 teaspoon nutmeg

Instructions:

1. Preheat the oven to 325°F (160°C) and grease a springform pan.
2. In a large bowl, mix the sourdough discard, flour, butter, and sugar until a crumbly dough forms. Press into the bottom of the springform pan and bake for 10 minutes.
3. In another bowl, beat together the cream cheese, sugar, eggs, vanilla, pumpkin puree, cinnamon, and nutmeg until smooth.
4. Pour the filling over the pre-baked crust and bake for 50-60 minutes until set.
5. Let cool completely before serving.

20. Sourdough Discard Raspberry Danish

👥 8 | ⏱ 30 min | 🍲 25 min

These flaky raspberry danishes are made with a sourdough discard pastry and filled with a sweet raspberry jam and cream cheese filling.

Ingredients:

- 1 cup sourdough discard
- 2 cups all-purpose flour
- 1/2 cup cold butter, cubed
- 1/4 cup cold water
- 1/2 teaspoon salt

For the Filling:

- 1/2 cup cream cheese, softened
- 1/4 cup powdered sugar
- 1/2 cup raspberry jam

Instructions:

1. In a large bowl, mix the sourdough discard, flour, butter, water, and salt until a dough forms. Chill for 30 minutes.
2. Preheat the oven to 375°F (190°C) and line a baking sheet with parchment paper.
3. Roll out the dough into a large rectangle and cut into 8 squares.
4. In a bowl, mix the cream cheese and powdered sugar until smooth. Spoon a small amount of the cream cheese mixture and raspberry jam onto each square.
5. Fold the corners of the dough over the filling and press to seal.
6. Bake for 20-25 minutes until golden.

21. Sourdough Discard Gingerbread Cookies

👥 24 cookies | ⏱ 15 min | 🍲 12 min

Spiced gingerbread cookies with a soft interior and a hint of sourdough tang, perfect for the holidays.

Ingredients:

- 1 cup sourdough discard
- 2 1/2 cups all-purpose flour
- 1/2 cup unsalted butter, softened
- 1/2 cup brown sugar
- 1/2 cup molasses
- 1 large egg
- 1 teaspoon ginger
- 1 teaspoon cinnamon
- 1/4 teaspoon nutmeg
- 1/4 teaspoon cloves
- 1/2 teaspoon baking soda
- 1/4 teaspoon salt

Instructions:

1. Preheat the oven to 350°F (175°C) and line a baking sheet with parchment paper.
2. In a large bowl, cream together butter and brown sugar. Mix in the sourdough discard, molasses, and egg.
3. In another bowl, whisk together flour, ginger, cinnamon, nutmeg, cloves, baking soda, and salt. Gradually add the dry ingredients to the wet.
4. Roll out the dough and cut into shapes. Bake for 10-12 minutes until firm.
5. Cool completely before decorating.

22. Sourdough Discard Fruitcake

👥 8 | ⏱ 30 min | 🍲 1 hr 15 min

A festive fruitcake packed with dried fruit, nuts, and spices, enhanced by the sourdough discard.

Ingredients:

- 1 cup sourdough discard
- 1 1/2 cups all-purpose flour
- 1/2 cup brown sugar
- 1/2 cup unsalted butter, softened
- 3 large eggs
- 1/4 cup orange juice
- 1 teaspoon cinnamon
- 1/2 teaspoon nutmeg
- 1/4 teaspoon cloves
- 1/2 cup raisins
- 1/2 cup dried apricots, chopped
- 1/2 cup dried cranberries
- 1/4 cup chopped walnuts

Instructions:

1. Preheat the oven to 325°F (160°C) and grease a loaf pan.
2. In a bowl, cream together the butter and brown sugar. Mix in the eggs, sourdough discard, and orange juice.
3. In another bowl, whisk together flour, cinnamon, nutmeg, and cloves. Combine the dry ingredients with the wet and fold in the dried fruits and walnuts.
4. Pour into the loaf pan and bake for 1 hour 15 minutes, or until a toothpick comes out clean.
5. Cool before serving.

23. Sourdough Discard Pumpkin Pie Tartlets

👥 12 tartlets | ⏱ 20 min | 🍲 30 min

Mini pumpkin pies in tart form, made with a sourdough discard crust and creamy pumpkin filling.

Ingredients:

- 1 cup sourdough discard
- 1 1/2 cups all-purpose flour
- 1/2 cup cold butter, cubed
- 1/4 cup cold water
- 1 cup pumpkin puree

- 1/4 cup brown sugar
- 1/2 teaspoon cinnamon
- 1/4 teaspoon nutmeg
- 1/4 teaspoon ginger
- 1/2 cup heavy cream
- 1 large egg

Instructions:

1. Preheat the oven to 350°F (175°C).
2. In a bowl, mix sourdough discard, flour, and cold butter until crumbly. Add cold water and form a dough. Roll out and cut into small circles, pressing into mini tart pans.
3. In another bowl, mix pumpkin puree, brown sugar, cinnamon, nutmeg, ginger, cream, and egg. Fill each tart shell with the pumpkin mixture.
4. Bake for 25-30 minutes until set. Cool before serving.

24. Sourdough Discard Apple Crumble

👥 6 | ⏱ 15 min | 🍲 30 min

A cozy dessert of warm baked apples topped with a sourdough discard crumble.

Ingredients:

- 1/2 cup sourdough discard
- 4 large apples, peeled and sliced
- 1/4 cup granulated sugar
- 1/2 teaspoon cinnamon
- 1/4 teaspoon nutmeg
- 1 cup all-purpose flour
- 1/2 cup brown sugar
- 1/4 cup cold butter, cubed

Instructions:

1. Preheat the oven to 375°F (190°C) and grease a baking dish.
2. Toss the apple slices with granulated sugar, cinnamon, and nutmeg. Spread them in the baking dish.

3. In a bowl, mix sourdough discard, flour, brown sugar, and cold butter until crumbly. Sprinkle over the apples.
4. Bake for 25-30 minutes until the topping is golden and the apples are tender.

25. Sourdough Discard Christmas Stollen

👥 8 | ⏱ 30 min | 🍲 45 min

A traditional German holiday bread filled with dried fruits, marzipan, and a touch of sourdough discard.

Ingredients:

- 1 cup sourdough discard
- 2 cups all-purpose flour
- 1/4 cup granulated sugar
- 1/2 cup warm milk
- 1/4 cup unsalted butter, melted
- 2 large eggs
- 1 teaspoon instant yeast
- 1/2 teaspoon cinnamon
- 1/2 cup raisins
- 1/4 cup chopped dried cherries
- 1/4 cup chopped almonds
- 1/4 cup marzipan

Instructions:

1. In a large bowl, mix sourdough discard, flour, sugar, milk, melted butter, eggs, yeast, and cinnamon. Knead for 8-10 minutes until smooth. Let rise for 1 hour.
2. Roll out the dough and spread with raisins, cherries, and almonds. Place marzipan in the center and fold the dough over it.
3. Let rise for another 30 minutes. Preheat the oven to 350°F (175°C) and bake for 40-45 minutes until golden brown.

26. Sourdough Discard Chocolate Babka

👥 8 | ⏱ 30 min | 🍲 35 min

A sweet and rich chocolate-filled babka, perfect for special occasions.

Ingredients:

- 1 cup sourdough discard
- 3 cups all-purpose flour
- 1/4 cup granulated sugar
- 1/2 cup warm milk
- 1/4 cup butter, melted
- 2 large eggs
- 1 teaspoon instant yeast
- 1/2 teaspoon salt

For the Filling:

- 1/2 cup chocolate spread (or Nutella)
- 1/4 cup chopped dark chocolate
- 1/4 cup chopped nuts (optional)

Instructions:

1. In a large bowl, mix sourdough discard, flour, sugar, warm milk, melted butter, eggs, yeast, and salt until a dough forms.
2. Knead for about 10 minutes until smooth and elastic. Let rise for 1-2 hours.
3. Roll out the dough into a large rectangle. Spread the chocolate filling evenly over the dough and sprinkle with chocolate chunks and nuts.
4. Roll the dough tightly into a log, then slice the log in half lengthwise. Twist the two pieces together and place in a greased loaf pan.
5. Let rise for another 30 minutes. Preheat the oven to 350°F (175°C).
6. Bake for 30-35 minutes until golden and cooked through.

27. Sourdough Discard Panettone

👥 8 | ⏱ 40 min | 🍲 1 hr

A traditional Italian Christmas bread with candied fruits, made extra light and fluffy with sourdough discard.

Ingredients:

- 1 cup sourdough discard
- 3 cups all-purpose flour
- 1/4 cup granulated sugar
- 1/2 cup warm milk
- 1/4 cup unsalted butter, softened
- 3 large eggs
- 1 teaspoon instant yeast
- 1/2 cup candied orange peel
- 1/2 cup raisins
- 1 teaspoon vanilla extract

Instructions:

1. In a bowl, mix sourdough discard, flour, sugar, milk, butter, eggs, yeast, and vanilla. Knead until smooth. Let rise for 1-2 hours.
2. Stir in the candied orange peel and raisins. Shape the dough into a round and place in a greased panettone mold or a deep baking dish.
3. Let rise again for 1 hour. Preheat the oven to 350°F (175°C) and bake for 45-60 minutes until golden.

28. Sourdough Discard Pecan Pie

👥 8 | ⏱ 20 min | 🍲 50 min

A rich, gooey pecan pie with a sourdough discard crust.

Ingredients:

- 1 cup sourdough discard
- 1 1/2 cups all-purpose flour

- 1/2 cup cold butter, cubed
- 1/4 cup cold water
- 1 cup pecans, chopped
- 3/4 cup brown sugar
- 1/2 cup corn syrup
- 1/4 cup butter, melted
- 3 large eggs
- 1 teaspoon vanilla extract

Instructions:

1. Preheat the oven to 350°F (175°C).
2. Mix sourdough discard, flour, and cold butter until crumbly. Add cold water and form a dough. Press into a pie dish.
3. In a separate bowl, whisk together brown sugar, corn syrup, melted butter, eggs, and vanilla. Stir in the pecans.
4. Pour the filling into the pie crust and bake for 50-60 minutes until set.

29. Sourdough Discard Chocolate Éclairs

👥 12 éclairs | ⏱ 25 min | 🍽 30 min

Light and airy éclairs filled with pastry cream and topped with chocolate glaze.

Ingredients:

- 1 cup sourdough discard
- 1/2 cup water
- 1/2 cup milk
- 1/2 cup butter
- 1 tablespoon sugar
- 1 cup all-purpose flour
- 4 large eggs

For the Filling:

- 1 cup milk
- 1/4 cup sugar
- 2 large egg yolks
- 1 tablespoon cornstarch
- 1 teaspoon vanilla extract

For the Glaze:

- 1/2 cup dark chocolate, melted
- 1/4 cup heavy cream

Instructions:

1. Preheat the oven to 400°F (200°C).
2. In a saucepan, heat the water, milk, butter, and sugar until boiling. Stir in the sourdough discard and flour until smooth. Remove from heat and beat in the eggs one at a time.
3. Pipe the dough onto a baking sheet in 4-inch strips and bake for 25-30 minutes.
4. For the filling, heat the milk in a saucepan. In a bowl, whisk the egg yolks, sugar, and cornstarch. Slowly pour the hot milk into the egg mixture, then return to the saucepan and cook until thickened.
5. Once the éclairs are cool, fill them with the pastry cream.
6. For the glaze, heat the chocolate and cream together until smooth. Dip the tops of the éclairs in the glaze.

30. Sourdough Discard Holiday Sugar Cookies

👥 24 cookies | ⏱ 10 min | 🍽 12 min

Classic sugar cookies made festive with a hint of sourdough discard, perfect for decorating during the holidays.

Ingredients:

- 1/2 cup sourdough discard
- 2 1/2 cups all-purpose flour
- 1/2 cup unsalted butter, softened
- 1/2 cup granulated sugar
- 1 large egg
- 1 teaspoon vanilla extract
- 1/2 teaspoon baking powder
- 1/4 teaspoon salt

Instructions:

1. Preheat the oven to 350°F (175°C) and line a baking sheet with parchment paper.

2. In a bowl, cream together the butter and sugar until light and fluffy. Mix in the sourdough discard, egg, and vanilla extract.
3. In another bowl, whisk together the flour, baking powder, and salt. Gradually add to the wet ingredients and mix until combined.
4. Roll out the dough on a floured surface and cut into shapes with cookie cutters.
5. Bake for 10-12 minutes until lightly golden. Cool before decorating with icing or sprinkles.

Chapter 9 - 28-Days Zero-Waste Meal Plan

The key to adopting a zero-waste approach in the kitchen is thoughtful planning and using ingredients to their fullest. This 28-day meal plan will help you maximize the use of sourdough discard and other common kitchen leftovers. Each week, you'll focus on meals that reduce waste, are easy to prepare, and are packed with flavor.

Week 1:

Day 1

- **Breakfast**: Fluffy Sourdough Pancakes (Page 16)
- **Lunch**: Sourdough Discard Veggie Burgers (Page 49)
- **Dinner**: Sourdough Discard Flatbread (Page 29)
- **Snack**: Sourdough Discard Crackers (Page 29)

Day 2

- **Breakfast**: Banana Sourdough Muffins (Page 16)
- **Lunch**: Sourdough Discard Veggie Burgers (Page 49)
- **Dinner**: Sourdough Discard Shepherd's Pie (Page 52)
- **Snack**: Sourdough Discard Cheese Crackers (Page 38)

Day 3

- **Breakfast**: Morning Glory Sourdough Muffins (Page 17)
- **Lunch**: Sourdough Discard Chicken Pot Pie (Page 49)
- **Dinner**: Sourdough Discard Fish Tacos (Page 54)
- **Snack**: Sourdough Discard Parmesan Crackers (Page 40)

Day 4

- **Breakfast**: Sourdough Waffles (Page 17)
- **Lunch**: Sourdough Discard Gnocchi (Page 50)
- **Dinner**: Sourdough Discard Veggie Stir-Fry (Page 59)
- **Snack**: Sourdough Discard Soft Pretzel Bites (Page 38)

Day 5

- **Breakfast**: Cinnamon Sourdough Rolls (Page 17)
- **Lunch**: Sourdough Discard Veggie Wraps (Page 57)

- **Dinner**: Sourdough Discard BBQ Chicken Pizza (Page 54)
- **Snack**: Sourdough Discard Garlic Breadsticks (Page 47)

Day 6

- **Breakfast**: Sourdough Discard English Muffins (Page 18)
- **Lunch**: Sourdough Discard Tomato Soup (Page 57)
- **Dinner**: Sourdough Discard Pork Buns (Page 55)
- **Snack**: Sourdough Discard Mozzarella Sticks (Page 42)

Day 7

- **Breakfast**: Sourdough Breakfast Pizza (Page 19)
- **Lunch**: Sourdough Discard Lasagna (Page 59)
- **Dinner**: Sourdough Discard Beef Stroganoff (Page 55)
- **Snack**: Sourdough Discard Onion Rings (Page 39)

Week 2:

Day 8

- **Breakfast**: Sourdough Discard Bagels (Page 19)
- **Lunch**: Sourdough Discard Chicken Salad (Page 58)
- **Dinner**: Sourdough Discard Flatbread (Page 29)
- **Snack**: Sourdough Discard Savory Crackers (Page 45)

Day 9

- **Breakfast**: Sourdough Discard Frittata (Page 19)
- **Lunch**: Sourdough Discard Stuffed Bell Peppers (Page 51)
- **Dinner**: Sourdough Discard Beef Wellington (Page 56)
- **Snack**: Sourdough Discard Spinach Artichoke Dip Bites (Page 43

Day 10

- **Breakfast**: Sourdough Discard Blueberry Pancakes (Page 20)
- **Lunch**: Sourdough Discard Veggie Quesadillas (Page 56)
- **Dinner**: Sourdough Discard Chicken and Dumplings (Page 54)
- **Snack**: Sourdough Discard Pesto Pinwheels (Page 45)

Day 11

- **Breakfast**: Sourdough Discard Coffee Cake (Page 20)
- **Lunch**: Sourdough Discard Spinach Lasagna (Page 51)
- **Dinner**: Sourdough Discard Beef Tacos (Page 63)
- **Snack**: Sourdough Discard Cheese Straws (Page 44)

Day 12

- **Breakfast**: Sourdough Discard Donuts (Page 21)
- **Lunch**: Sourdough Discard Veggie Burgers (Page 49)
- **Dinner**: Sourdough Discard Turkey Meatballs (Page 62)
- **Snack**: Sourdough Discard Empanadas (Page 41)

Day 13

- **Breakfast**: Sourdough Discard Granola (Page 21)
- **Lunch**: Sourdough Discard Chicken Enchiladas (Page 53)
- **Dinner**: Sourdough Discard Fish Tacos (Page 54)
- **Snack**: Sourdough Discard Zucchini Fritters (Page 38)

Day 14

- **Breakfast**: Sourdough Discard Scones (Page 22)
- **Lunch**: Sourdough Discard Spinach Quiche (Page 59)
- **Dinner**: Sourdough Discard Flatbread Pizza (Page 52)
- **Snack**: Sourdough Discard Sausage Rolls (Page 44)

Week 3:

Day 15

- **Breakfast**: Sourdough Discard Omelette with Herbed Crust (Page 22)
- **Lunch**: Sourdough Discard Tomato Soup (Page 57)
- **Dinner**: Sourdough Discard Beef Stroganoff (Page 55)
- **Snack**: Sourdough Discard Parmesan Crackers (Page 40)

Day 16

- **Breakfast**: Sourdough Discard Apple Cinnamon Loaf (Page 22)
- **Lunch**: Sourdough Discard Veggie Quesadillas (Page 56)

- **Dinner**: Sourdough Discard Chicken and Dumplings (Page 54)
- **Snack**: Sourdough Discard Savory Crackers (Page 45)

Day 17

- **Breakfast**: Sourdough Discard Dutch Baby (Page 23)
- **Lunch**: Sourdough Discard Chicken Salad (Page 58)
- **Dinner**: Sourdough Discard Shepherd's Pie (Page 52)
- **Snack**: Sourdough Discard Zucchini Fritters (Page 38)

Day 18

- **Breakfast**: Sourdough Discard Pumpkin Spice Scones (Page 23)
- **Lunch**: Sourdough Discard Spinach Lasagna (Page 51)
- **Dinner**: Sourdough Discard Stuffed Bell Peppers (Page 51)
- **Snack**: Sourdough Discard Empanadas (Page 41)

Day 19

- **Breakfast**: Sourdough Discard Apple Pancakes (Page 23)
- **Lunch**: Sourdough Discard Chicken Enchiladas (Page 53)
- **Dinner**: Sourdough Discard Beef Tacos (Page 63)
- **Snack**: Sourdough Discard Spinach Artichoke Dip Bites (Page 43)

Day 20

- **Breakfast**: Sourdough Discard Granola Bars (Page 24)
- **Lunch**: Sourdough Discard Veggie Burgers (Page 49)
- **Dinner**: Sourdough Discard Fish Tacos (Page 54)
- **Snack**: Sourdough Discard Cheese Crackers (Page 38)

Day 21

- **Breakfast**: Sourdough Discard Sweet Potato Hash (Page 24)
- **Lunch**: Sourdough Discard Stuffed Bell Peppers (Page 51)
- **Dinner**: Sourdough Discard Pork Buns (Page 55)
- **Snack**: Sourdough Discard Mozzarella Sticks (Page 42)

Week 4:

Day 22

- **Breakfast**: Sourdough Discard Chia Pudding (Page 24)
- **Lunch**: Sourdough Discard Veggie Wraps (Page 57)
- **Dinner**: Sourdough Discard Chicken Pot Pie (Page 49)
- **Snack**: Sourdough Discard Spinach Dip Bread Bowl (Page 39)

Day 23

- **Breakfast**: Sourdough Discard Spinach Feta Muffins (Page 25)
- **Lunch**: Sourdough Discard Falafel (Page 58)
- **Dinner**: Sourdough Discard Shepherd's Pie (Page 52)
- **Snack**: Sourdough Discard Pesto Pinwheels (Page 45)

Day 24

- **Breakfast**: Sourdough Discard Breakfast Burritos (Page 25)
- **Lunch**: Sourdough Discard Veggie Tacos (Page 50)
- **Dinner**: Sourdough Discard Meatloaf (Page 52)
- **Snack**: Sourdough Discard Garlic Parmesan Breadsticks (Page 39)

Day 25

- **Breakfast**: Sourdough Discard Oatmeal (Page 25)
- **Lunch**: Sourdough Discard Chicken Enchiladas (Page 53)
- **Dinner**: Sourdough Discard Veggie Stir-Fry (Page 59)
- **Snack**: Sourdough Discard Empanadas (Page 41)

Day 26

- **Breakfast**: Sourdough Discard Waffles (Page 26)
- **Lunch**: Sourdough Discard Quiche (Page 53)
- **Dinner**: Sourdough Discard Chicken and Dumplings (Page 54)
- **Snack**: Sourdough Discard Cheese Crackers (Page 38)

Day 27

- **Breakfast**: Sourdough Discard Veggie Frittata (Page 26)
- **Lunch**: Sourdough Discard Tomato Soup (Page 57)

- **Dinner**: Sourdough Discard BBQ Chicken Pizza (Page 54)
- **Snack**: Sourdough Discard Mozzarella Sticks (Page 42)

Day 28

- **Breakfast**: Sourdough Discard Breakfast Skillet (Page 26)
- **Lunch**: Sourdough Discard Veggie Wraps (Page 57)
- **Dinner**: Sourdough Discard Pork Buns (Page 55)
- **Snack**: Sourdough Discard Garlic Breadsticks (Page 47)

Chapter 10: Frequently Asked Questions

1. What is sourdough discard?

Sourdough discard is the portion of sourdough starter that is removed during the feeding process to maintain a healthy and active starter. It contains flour and water and is often discarded, but it can be repurposed in recipes like those found in this cookbook.

2. Do I need a sourdough starter to use the recipes in this book?

Yes, many of the recipes rely on sourdough discard, which comes from maintaining a sourdough starter. However, creating a sourdough starter is simple and requires only flour and water. If you don't already have one, there are plenty of resources available to guide you through the process of starting and feeding it.

3. How do I store sourdough discard?

You can store sourdough discard in the refrigerator in an airtight container for up to a week. For longer storage, you can freeze it in portions and thaw it as needed for your recipes.

4. Can I use gluten-free flour in these recipes?

Most of the recipes in this book are designed for regular wheat-based sourdough discard. However, we include a section of gluten-free sourdough discard recipes for those who maintain a gluten-free sourdough starter.

5. How do I know if my sourdough discard is still good?

If your sourdough discard smells strongly of alcohol or has mold on it, it's best to discard it. However, a tangy, slightly sour smell is normal, and that means it's still good to use in recipes.

6. Are these recipes difficult or time-consuming?

The recipes in this book are designed with busy individuals in mind. Many of them are quick and easy, with clear instructions that don't require advanced baking skills. Additionally, the book includes time-saving tips and six exclusive bonuses to make the process even simpler.

7. Can I substitute ingredients in the recipes?

Yes, many recipes are flexible, and we encourage you to adapt them based on what you have available. For example, you can swap different vegetables, cheeses, or herbs depending on your preferences and pantry.

8. What's the best way to prevent food waste when using sourdough discard?

One of the key goals of this cookbook is to help you minimize food waste by utilizing sourdough discard in creative ways. We recommend storing your discard in the fridge and planning your meals around the recipes in this book to ensure that none of it goes to waste.

9. Can I use the recipes in this book if I'm new to sourdough baking?

Absolutely! While some recipes involve more advanced techniques, many are beginner-friendly. The book also includes bonus guides, such as a sourdough troubleshooting section and starter tips, to help you succeed in sourdough baking.

10. How do I make a sourdough starter if I don't have one?

Making a sourdough starter is simple. All you need is flour and water. Combine equal parts flour and water, mix thoroughly, and let it sit at room temperature. Feed the starter daily by discarding half of it and adding fresh flour and water. Within a week, your starter should be active and ready for baking.

11. Can I freeze the baked goods made with sourdough discard?

Yes, most baked goods made with sourdough discard can be frozen. Simply cool the items completely, wrap them tightly in plastic wrap or place them in an airtight container, and freeze. Thaw them at room temperature or reheat in the oven when you're ready to enjoy.

12. What are the benefits of using sourdough discard in recipes?

Sourdough discard adds a unique flavor to baked goods, often giving them a tangy complexity. It also helps reduce food waste by repurposing what would otherwise be thrown away. Additionally, sourdough discard can improve the texture of certain recipes, making them fluffier or chewier.

13. Can I bake with discard that hasn't been fed recently?

Yes, you can use sourdough discard that hasn't been recently fed. In fact, the recipes in this book are designed to work with "unfed" discard, meaning it doesn't need to be freshly activated. Just make sure your discard is stored properly in the fridge and doesn't smell off.

14. How do I know if my sourdough starter is healthy?

A healthy sourdough starter should have a slightly tangy, pleasant smell and a bubbly, airy texture. If your starter smells unpleasant (like rotten food) or has developed mold, it's best to start over.

15. Can I make adjustments to the serving sizes in the recipes?

Yes, most recipes can be scaled up or down to fit your needs. Simply adjust the ingredient quantities proportionally based on how many servings you want to make.

16. What are some creative ways to use sourdough discard aside from baking?

In addition to baked goods, sourdough discard can be used in pancakes, waffles, pizza dough, crackers, and even as a thickener in soups and stews. This book is filled with ideas to help you get the most out of your discard.

17. How do I make my sourdough starter more or less tangy?

The tanginess of your sourdough starter is influenced by how often you feed it and the temperature at which it's kept. To make it more tangy, allow the starter to sit longer between feedings. For a milder flavor, feed it more frequently and keep it in a cooler environment.

18. Can I use sourdough discard in non-baked dishes?

Yes! While most people associate sourdough discard with baked goods, you can also use it to make batters for frying, thickening sauces, or even in savory dishes like quiches and frittatas.

19. How do I prevent my sourdough discard from going to waste if I can't bake right away?

If you can't bake immediately, you can freeze your discard in small portions and thaw it as needed for recipes. This way, you always have discard ready when you're ready to bake.

20. Are there recipes in this book that are kid-friendly?

Yes, many of the recipes are designed to be family-friendly, including options like pizza, pancakes, and cookies that are sure to please both kids and adults.

Chapter 11: Sustainable Practices in the Kitchen

In a world where sustainability is becoming increasingly important, the kitchen is one of the best places to start implementing eco-friendly habits. By making small but meaningful changes, you can significantly reduce your kitchen's environmental impact without sacrificing the joy of cooking or the quality of your meals. In this chapter, we'll explore simple, effective strategies to help you cook more sustainably, reduce waste, conserve resources, and make your kitchen a greener, more efficient space.

1. Plan Your Meals to Minimize Waste

Meal planning is one of the most effective ways to reduce food waste and save time. When you plan your meals in advance, you can purchase only what you need and ensure that ingredients are used in multiple dishes, reducing the likelihood of forgotten leftovers or unused produce.

Tips for Effective Meal Planning:

- **Use a meal planner**: Schedule your meals for the week using a meal planner. This ensures you utilize perishable items and prevent food from spoiling.
- **Shop smart**: Make a grocery list based on your meal plan, and stick to it. Avoid impulse buys, especially of items that spoil quickly.
- **Batch cooking**: Prepare meals in bulk and freeze portions for future use. This not only saves time but ensures that no ingredients go to waste.

2. Utilize All Parts of Ingredients

A key part of sustainable cooking is learning how to use every part of your ingredients. Many people throw away perfectly edible parts of fruits and vegetables, but with a little creativity, these can be turned into delicious meals.

Ideas for Utilizing All Parts:

- **Vegetable scraps for broth**: Save vegetable peels, stalks, and ends in the freezer. Once you have enough, make a flavorful vegetable broth.
- **Use citrus peels**: Lemon and orange peels can be zested and used to flavor baked goods, drinks, or salads. They can also be candied for a sweet treat.
- **Stale bread**: Don't throw away stale bread! Turn it into breadcrumbs, croutons, or use it in bread pudding or stuffing.
- **Leftover coffee grounds**: Coffee grounds can be used in composting, as a natural cleaner for pots and pans, or even in desserts like coffee-flavored cakes.

3. Choose Sustainable Ingredients

Selecting sustainable ingredients is another vital step in reducing your kitchen's environmental footprint. This involves considering how the food was grown, transported, and processed.

How to Choose Sustainable Ingredients:

- **Buy local**: Purchasing local produce reduces the carbon footprint associated with transportation and supports your local economy.

- **Seasonal eating**: Focus on ingredients that are in season. These are often fresher, more affordable, and have a lower environmental impact due to reduced transportation and storage needs.

- **Opt for organic when possible**: Organic farming practices are better for the environment, as they avoid harmful pesticides and promote soil health.

- **Plant-based options**: While you don't have to become vegetarian, incorporating more plant-based meals can reduce your carbon footprint, as plant-based foods generally require fewer resources than meat and dairy products.

4. Smart Storage Solutions

Proper storage is essential for keeping food fresh longer, which helps to reduce waste and avoid unnecessary trips to the grocery store.

Best Practices for Food Storage:

- **Invest in airtight containers**: Use glass or BPA-free containers to store leftovers and cut produce. This helps to keep food fresh and avoid spoilage.

- **Label and date**: When storing leftovers or pre-prepared ingredients, always label them with the date. This will help you keep track of when items should be used or frozen.

- **Use reusable beeswax wraps**: Instead of plastic wrap, opt for reusable beeswax wraps. These are eco-friendly and can be used to cover bowls, wrap sandwiches, or keep produce fresh.

- **Compost when possible**: If food does spoil or is inedible (like eggshells or coffee grounds), compost it instead of throwing it in the trash. Composting reduces landfill waste and creates nutrient-rich soil for gardening.

5. Energy-Efficient Cooking

Cooking requires a lot of energy, but there are simple ways to reduce the amount used without compromising on the quality of your meals.

Energy-Efficient Cooking Tips:

- **Batch cooking**: Cook multiple meals at once to make the most of your oven or stovetop's heat.

- **Use the right-sized cookware**: Using a small pan on a large burner wastes energy. Always match your cookware to the burner size.

- **Cover pots and pans**: Covering your pots and pans when cooking traps heat, reducing cooking time and saving energy.

- **Turn off the oven early**: Turn off your oven a few minutes before your food is fully cooked. The residual heat will finish the cooking process, saving energy.

- **Opt for energy-efficient appliances**: When it's time to replace old kitchen appliances, look for Energy Star-rated options. These use significantly less energy than older models.

6. Cook from Scratch

Cooking from scratch not only tastes better, but it also helps reduce your reliance on processed and pre-packaged foods, which often come with excessive packaging waste.

Why Cooking from Scratch is Sustainable:

- **Reduces packaging waste**: Pre-packaged foods typically come in plastic, which contributes to landfill waste. By cooking from scratch, you can use fresh ingredients and avoid unnecessary packaging.
- **Control ingredients**: Cooking from scratch allows you to choose healthier, more sustainable ingredients without preservatives or artificial additives.
- **More eco-friendly**: Making your own staples like bread, yogurt, or sauces reduces the energy and resources needed to produce and transport store-bought versions.

7. Water Conservation

Water is one of the most precious resources, and it's essential to conserve it wherever possible in the kitchen.

Water Conservation Tips:

- **Don't leave the tap running**: Whether you're washing vegetables or doing dishes, turn off the tap when water isn't needed.
- **Use a dishwasher**: Running a full dishwasher uses less water than washing dishes by hand. If washing by hand, use a basin of water instead of running water continuously.
- **Reuse water**: Collect the water used to rinse fruits and vegetables, and use it to water plants or for cleaning.
- **Steam instead of boil**: Steaming vegetables uses less water than boiling and retains more nutrients.

8. Reduce Single-Use Plastics

Reducing single-use plastics is one of the most impactful ways to make your kitchen more sustainable.

Alternatives to Single-Use Plastics:

- **Reusable shopping bags**: Bring your own cloth or canvas bags when shopping to avoid plastic grocery bags.
- **Glass containers**: Store food in reusable glass containers instead of plastic ones.
- **Silicone storage bags**: Replace plastic sandwich and freezer bags with reusable silicone bags.

Chapter 11: Sustainable Practices in the Kitchen

- **Metal or bamboo straws**: Instead of single-use plastic straws, opt for reusable metal or bamboo alternatives.
- **Buy in bulk**: Purchasing pantry staples in bulk reduces packaging waste and is often more economical.

9. Use Energy-Efficient Lighting

The lighting in your kitchen can also be a source of energy waste, but switching to energy-efficient options can make a big difference.

Tips for Energy-Efficient Lighting:

- **Use LED bulbs**: LED lights use significantly less energy and last longer than traditional incandescent bulbs.
- **Install motion sensors or timers**: If you often forget to turn off kitchen lights, consider installing motion sensors or timers to automatically turn off the lights when the kitchen isn't in use.

10. Grow Your Own Herbs and Vegetables

Growing your own herbs or vegetables, even on a small scale, can reduce your reliance on store-bought produce and cut down on packaging and transportation waste.

Benefits of Growing Your Own Produce:

- **Fresh and organic**: You have full control over what you grow, ensuring your herbs and vegetables are organic and pesticide-free.
- **Less waste**: You can harvest only what you need, reducing the chance of produce going bad before you use it.
- **Eco-friendly**: Growing your own food reduces the environmental impact associated with transporting produce from farms to stores.

Chapter 12: Conclusion – Your Journey to Zero-Waste Cooking

Congratulations! By reaching this point in the book, you've taken the first crucial steps toward a more sustainable, zero-waste kitchen. Throughout the recipes, meal plans, and tips provided, you've learned how to turn what would have once been discarded—like sourdough starter waste—into delicious, resourceful meals. But this is only the beginning of your journey.

Zero-waste cooking is not just about reducing what goes into the trash; it's about embracing a new mindset. It's a way of approaching the kitchen with creativity, mindfulness, and a sense of purpose. Every leftover, every scrap of food, every sourdough discard can be seen as an opportunity. An opportunity to make something nourishing, to feed yourself and your loved ones, and to contribute to a more sustainable planet.

What You've Learned: Key Takeaways

Sourdough Discard is a Treasure: You now know that sourdough discard can be more than just a byproduct of sourdough baking. It's a versatile ingredient that can be used in everything from breakfast pancakes to savory dinners and sweet treats. This knowledge alone can help you reduce waste and add delicious variety to your meals.

Meal Planning is Essential: With the 28-day meal plan, you've seen firsthand how planning your meals can help you avoid food waste. By organizing your week, using leftovers creatively, and repurposing ingredients, you're able to maximize what you have on hand and avoid unnecessary trips to the store.

Sustainability is a Lifestyle: Sustainable practices in the kitchen extend beyond just cooking. From thoughtful grocery shopping to smart food storage, you've learned how small changes—like growing your own herbs, buying seasonal produce, and storing food correctly—can make a significant difference in your environmental impact.

Creativity in the Kitchen: Zero-waste cooking encourages innovation. Whether it's making a soup out of vegetable scraps or turning stale bread into croutons, you've discovered how to get creative with ingredients and turn potential waste into something delicious.

Keep the Momentum Going

Your journey doesn't stop here. Cooking sustainably is a continuous process of learning and adapting. As you become more comfortable with these practices, you'll find new ways to further reduce waste in your kitchen. Here are some tips to keep you inspired:

Experiment with New Recipes: Don't be afraid to take risks. Try out new recipes with your sourdough discard or invent your own. Challenge yourself to use every part of your ingredients in unexpected ways.

Share Your Knowledge: Invite friends and family to join you on your zero-waste journey. Host a sourdough discard baking day or share leftover-based meal ideas. The more people who adopt these practices, the greater the collective impact on reducing food waste.

Stay Curious: Continue to explore ways to improve your sustainability efforts. Whether it's composting, learning more about regenerative agriculture, or finding ways to reduce energy use in your kitchen, there is always more to learn.

A Movement Toward Mindfulness

Zero-waste cooking is about more than reducing your ecological footprint; it's about mindfulness. It's about being aware of the ingredients you use, how you source them, and how you can fully appreciate what nature provides. When you take a moment to pause and consider the journey of each ingredient—from farm to table—you become more connected to your food and the planet. You start to see value in things you might have once discarded, like the humble sourdough discard.

As you move forward, remember that every small change counts. Whether it's using leftovers in a new recipe, cutting down on food packaging, or simply being more mindful of what's in your fridge, each action contributes to a larger, collective effort to care for our planet.

The Next Steps

So, where do you go from here? Your journey to zero-waste cooking is ongoing, and there's always room for growth and improvement. Here are a few next steps to keep in mind as you continue this path:

Continue Planning: Keep utilizing meal planners and shopping lists to ensure you buy only what you need. Stick to seasonal and local ingredients when possible, as this helps reduce the environmental impact of transportation and promotes the use of fresh, in-season produce.

Reduce Waste Even Further: As you become more experienced with zero-waste cooking, try to reduce your reliance on store-bought, packaged goods. Learn to make your own staples, like homemade sauces, bread, or yogurt. Consider growing a small herb or vegetable garden to further reduce your reliance on store-bought items.

Embrace a Community: Whether online or in-person, there are communities of people who are passionate about zero-waste living and sustainability. Joining these groups can offer support, inspiration, and new ideas on how to continue minimizing waste in your kitchen.

Celebrate Your Progress: Finally, take a moment to reflect on how far you've come. It's important to celebrate the small victories, whether that's learning to make sourdough pancakes or finding ways to store food more efficiently. Every step toward zero-waste living is worth celebrating.

A Final Word

You've made the choice to cook in a way that honors the earth, values ingredients, and reduces waste. This is no small feat, and it will have a lasting impact not only on your kitchen but on the environment as well. The road to a zero-waste kitchen may not always be easy, but with creativity, mindfulness, and perseverance, you are contributing to a better future—one meal at a time.

Thank you for embarking on this journey. Keep cooking, keep experimenting, and most importantly, keep reducing waste. Your zero-waste kitchen is a testament to your dedication to sustainability, and we're excited to see where your culinary journey will take you next.

Happy zero-waste cooking!

Get your free bonuses

Discover a wealth of exclusive resources to elevate
your sourdough baking and embrace a more sustainable lifestyle!

Scan the QR code now to download them for free and start your journey:

Did you enjoy this book?

I hope this collection of " Sourdough Discard Recipes Cookbook"has inspired you and made your baking journey more enjoyable! Your feedback means the world to me, and hearing from readers like you helps me understand what you loved and how I can make future books even better.

If you found value in these recipes, I'd be thrilled if you could take a moment to leave a review on Amazon. Your positive review not only helps others discover the book, but it also supports the growth of this community of sourdough enthusiasts.

Leaving a review is quick and easy— Simply scan the QR code below to access a feedback form where you can share your thoughts, and favorite parts!

Your input helps me continue to grow and provide even better resources.

If you have ideas for improvement or any suggestions, I'd love to hear from you.

Thank you so much for your time and support!

Get your free bonuses

55703714R00059